Praise for *Contemplative Witnessing*

"Cindy Lee speaks to the grief that BIPOC communities feel at the loss of our sacred selves in a dominant Western system of colonization, colonialism, patriarchy, and missionarism. Through contemplative witnessing in community, Dr. Lee offers practical approaches by which we can restore our sacred wholeness and hold our BIPOC companionees in healing and change. As a BIPOC woman who co-coordinates Year One of a Spiritual Director formation program, I look to Dr. Lee as a trailblazer in our field."

—**Vel Roman**, cofacilitator and co-coordinator of The Art of Spiritual Direction, Stillpoint

"Bold, healing, and deeply moving, *Contemplative Witnessing* calls us to honor the sacred stories of BIPOC communities, sparking both personal and collective liberation. Cindy Lee invites us to reimagine seeing and listening as radical acts of witness, celebrating our sacred belovedness and belonging. She has a way of uncovering what's remained unwitnessed in you, freeing you to be seen in the fullness of your past, present, and future—fully divine and deeply connected. This book transforms how we encounter one another, the world, and even our own souls. Let it bear witness to your unfolding sacred story. Be uncomfortable and let yourself be transformed."

—**Brenda Bertrand**, chaplain, Fuller Theological Seminary

"Reading Cindy Lee's book feels like riding the breath of the Spirit as it flows into my heart, body, and soul, filling a deep longing. From a BIPOC-focused lens, Lee uses a rhizomatic approach that creatively enriches, challenges and expands what contemplative witnessing (spiritual direction) and communal care can be, and how these can guide all soul care practitioners in imagining new spiritual experiences and spaces. Through three movements—contemplative witnessing, sacred movements, and communal care—Lee uses her own experience and research as an Asian American practitioner to share stories of other BIPOC people, spiritual practices, probing questions, and other wisdom voices to bring this book alive. I am still resting with how she expands discernment by talking about ways of knowing and how sacred seeing leads to sacred responding in the face of injustice and harm. I wholeheartedly recommend this book for all involved in soul care work as a place of restoration and rest for BIPOC people and as a resource for all to expand their horizons, for people from many traditions or no tradition, formation programs, book clubs, spiritual practice circles, and many more. I will continue to linger with this book."

—**Ravi Verma**, former council chair, Spiritual Directors International

"Cindy S. Lee offers us a chance to see the genuine in ourselves from a widened scope. *Contemplative Witnessing* is a must-read as an important corrective to the typical Western, transactional, and individualized framework of spiritual care we hear on repeat. As she puts it so well, 'Sacred seeing in community allows our human dignity and belovedness to be witnessed and affirmed.' Few books I've read cover this area of spiritual formation with such skill and sensitivity as Lee does."

—**Lisa Colón DeLay**, author of *The Wild Land Within: Cultivating Wholeness through Spiritual Practice*

"From my perspective as a white man, spiritual director, and faculty member of Stillpoint's The Art of Spiritual Direction, *Contemplative Witnessing* is an essential guide and teacher for understanding and holding space for BIPOC spiritual companions and other marginalized folx in spiritual direction. I value Cindy S. Lee's voice, her ability to challenge normative culture and her compassionate and approachable narrative. This book is integral for spiritual directors and spiritual formation training for future spiritual directors."

—**Rick Sforza**, faculty in The Art of Spiritual Direction, Stillpoint

CONTEMPLATIVE WITNESSING

CONTEMPLATIVE WITNESSING

BIPOC-Centered Spiritual Direction

CINDY S. LEE

FORTRESS PRESS
MINNEAPOLIS

CONTEMPLATIVE WITNESSING
BIPOC-Centered Spiritual Direction

30 29 28 27 26 25 1 2 3 4 5 6 7 8 9

Library of Congress Cataloging-in-Publication Data

Names: Lee, Cindy S. (Sing-Yi), author.
Title: Contemplative witnessing : BIPOC-centered spiritual direction / Cindy S. Lee.
Description: Minneapolis : Fortress Press, 2025. | Includes bibliographical references.
Identifiers: LCCN 2024040958 (print) | LCCN 2024040959 (ebook) | ISBN 9798889833338 (print) | ISBN 9798889833345 (ebook)
Subjects: LCSH: Ethnicity--United States--Religious practice. | Race relations--United States. | Sexual minorities--United States--Religious practice. | Social justice--United States. | Marginality, Social--United States. | Spirituality--Christianity.
Classification: LCC BL65.E75 L44 2025 (print) | LCC BL65.E75 (ebook) | DDC 201/.76284--dc23/eng/20241206
LC record available at https://lccn.loc.gov/2024040958
LC ebook record available at https://lccn.loc.gov/2024040959

Cover design: Kristin Miller
Cover illustration: compilation of stock illustrations from Getty Images

Print ISBN: 979-8-8898-3333-8

eBook ISBN: 979-8-8898-3334-5

Contents

Preface

Enter In: A Guided Meditation for Decentering and Centering

Enter into your sacred space of prayer or meditation in whatever ways feel comfortable for your body. Take a few deep and slow breaths. With each breath allow your body, mind, and spirit to settle deeper into your sacred space to encounter your sacred self.

Decentering

Take a moment to ask gently: How have you centered whiteness? Or how have you centered dominant cultural or social experiences that are not your own? In the silence, allow for past or recent interactions and experiences to come to mind. Notice how those experiences feel in your body, emotions, and spirit.

Centering

Now take a moment to ask: How do you center your own cultural and embodied ways of being and knowing? Once

> again allow experiences and interactions to come to mind. In what ways do you center the wisdoms of your ancestors? In what ways do you embody the rituals and movements of your cultural traditions? Notice how it feels in your body, emotions, and spirit to center your own cultural ways of being.

I am committed to teach and write about spiritual direction from a BIPOC-centered perspective regardless of my audience. We have each, in varying ways, embodied a Western-centered posture to navigate the white, Western norm in our social systems and institutions. Our continual liberation means centering non-Western ways of being in our spiritualities and lived experiences without needing to explain or defend our ways. In this book I don't spend any time trying to prove that racism, colonization, and the violence of white supremacy exist in our societies. I am assuming that is true. This book moves the conversation forward to how we facilitate spiritual spaces of rest and healing for BIPOC communities that experience racism in our everyday lives.

I use the term *Black, Indigenous, and People of Color* (BIPOC) intentionally to recognize our interconnectedness. As a Taiwanese American, I can only speak and write from my Asian American experience in the United States. But my part in our collective is to recognize the deep level of systemic injustices that Black, Latine, and Indigenous communities experience in our country that are different from the racism

I may experience. As an Asian American, for our communal healing I equally prioritize Black, Indigenous, and Latine healing even as I advocate for the Asian American community. In reality, the term *BIPOC* represents a vast diversity of peoples that often get lumped together as a contrast to the power of white, Western normativity. We need to recognize the diversity and distinctiveness within people of color in the United States. We can't discover a non-Western spirituality unless we are asking what a liberating spirituality is for Black communities, for Latine communities, for Indigenous communities, for Asian communities, for Middle Eastern communities, for LGBTQIA+ communities, for disabled communities, and others. The responses to these questions will be very different. Even within Asian American communities the needs of Korean communities are different from the needs of Filipino communities or Indian communities. The distinctions and particularities of our cultural experiences are important. At the same time, the term *BIPOC* recognizes our interdependence. We need one another in our collective liberation.

Although this book centers the BIPOC experience, white readers are invited to listen to this conversation. For white readers, you are entering into an intentional practice of not being centered in this book. This decentering may feel awkward at first since you may have lived in a social context in which your experiences are the assumed norm. The purpose of this book is to re-form our bodies, minds, and spirits to intentionally decenter Western norms and expectations.

The Western model of one-on-one spiritual direction can be individualistic and transactional. I have a formal spiritual direction practice in which I'm paid, and I keep professional boundaries. I recognize the limitations of this practice and also see that it serves a purpose. At the same time, we are not limited by this Western model. We can look back to our ancestral traditions to find various forms of spiritual companioning relationships. We can also reimagine what this practice looks like communally and informally. I consider myself a spiritual director in practice and a spiritual companion in community. I hope how I show up with my directees with a listening presence is also how I show up with friends and my community. This helps me to live a congruent, integrated life where my practice is not separated from how I live my life. The training I've received is a gift I have to offer my community. I may offer my friends and community intentional listening spaces, especially in seasons of discernment or grief. Spiritual companioning in community is mutual. I must be open in allowing my community to offer the same listening presence to me.

As I look at spirituality with a BIPOC-centered lens, I explore here ways of facilitating the soul-work within communities of color. This book does not offer the only way of BIPOC-centered care. Instead, it represents my own learnings and lived experiences as a spiritual companion with people of color and as a teacher of spiritual direction. I fully believe that BIPOC communities need to immerse in our own cultural spiritualities in order to experience healing and restoration. We also need to experience our unique spiritualities in community with support and care. Therefore, a BIPOC-centered care is constantly evolving and changing as we each explore what that care feels like embodied in each of us.

Every culture has practices of communal spiritual care. As I commit to training more spiritual companions of color, I hope I keep learning from others the expansive possibilities of spiritual and communal care. To model this integration of our cultural traditions with our practices of spiritual care, this book also explores what my own Taiwanese tradition can teach us about our collective spirituality. I draw from ancestral and Daoist traditions as well as my own family's experiences and stories.

I hope this book expands our imaginations and creativities for how we can create new spiritual experiences and spaces together.

Acknowledgments

To the facilitators, alumni, and students of Liberated Together Spiritual Direction School for women of color, queer women of color, and nonbinary people of color: You continuously inspire me and expand my imaginations for community care. Special thanks to Erna, LeAnn, Puanani, Christina, and Chris.

In this book, I share a few of my own stories from my relationship with my spiritual director over the years. Rebekah, thank you for exemplifying a contemplative witness in my life.

I want to recognize the foundational works put together by the Spiritual Directors of Color Network. These works include *Embodied Spirits: Stories of Spiritual Directors of Color* and *Kaleidoscope: Broadening the Palette in the Art of Spiritual Direction*.[1] These edited works reflect the wisdoms from a variety of BIPOC spiritual directors. These works revealed to me that spiritual direction is not a one-size-fits-all experience. As each author shared their particular experiences, they affirmed to me that my cultural tradition and stories matter in how I show up both as a directee and a director.

Lastly, thank you to my editor, Yvonne, at Fortress Press for all the ways you have advocated for me. You have demonstrated to me the importance of having more women of color in the publishing industry.

Introduction

When I first began training as a spiritual director, spiritual direction was not something I planned to *do*, rather I saw in spiritual direction the kind of person I desire to *be*. My experiences in community, service, activism, and leadership had led to constant cycles of burnout. I felt depleted by obligations to serve others and respond to everyone's needs. As I attempted to help other people, I often carried the heaviness of their burdens and sufferings. I also navigated through painful conflicts and disappointments in leadership. I carried into relationships my own self-doubts and need for approval. All these experiences further inflamed my lifelong struggle with social anxiety. I longed for a healthier way of being with people. I saw in spiritual direction an intentional practice to cultivate a listening, nonanxious, and restful presence in myself, especially in the context of community.

I first experienced this listening presence as a participant in a contemplative small group. Each time a person spoke in the group, the group would honor what was spoken with a minute or two of silence before the next person spoke. There was no back-and-forth conversation, no critique or discussion, no answering of questions. The silences at first felt awkward and very long as we got used to the pattern of speaking, silence, speaking, silence, speaking, silence. Whenever I spoke, I felt self-conscious and vulnerable as my words felt weightier in the ensuing silence. But as I got used to this communal rhythm, I realized how it was slowly transforming my way of being present with this community. In that brief silence I learned to allow other people's experiences to be their own experience without feeling a need to help them or resolve their issues. Our honoring of each other's words communicated that we believed in each person's own agency and wisdom to come to our own resolutions. The silence helped move our words from the mental discussion space into our heart emotion space. I learned to be fully attentive to others when they spoke without being preoccupied with my own insecurities. I could wait for the silences in between to attune to myself and my own internal responses. I also learned to value my own words when it was my turn to speak, just as I honored the words of others. I knew that I needed to be further trained and formed in this way of being in community.

I define spiritual direction as a communal practice of contemplative witnessing. *Contemplation* can be defined as a sacred seeing as we gaze at the divine and receive the divine gaze on us. Through that divine gaze we see and experience our most sacred selves. Contemplation is often experienced through spiritual practices that help facilitate an honest look within. We can engage in contemplative practices through simple moments of silence or a walk immersed in nature. These practices help us to pause and take a step back from our everyday routines in order to connect with that honest, sacred gaze at our lives. Contemplation can also be experienced through extended practices like meditation or a pilgrimage. Extended practices can facilitate a deeper examining of our lives.

Contemplative witnessing, then, is a practice that facilitates this sacred seeing in community. It is a shared spiritual practice in which we enter into the soul space of others. I can meet the sacred self of another; someone they might not often reveal to others or even themselves. Together we compassionately and slowly nurture a deeper attunement to ourselves, to divine presence, and to the longings of our communities. Often, we think of spiritual practices like prayer and meditation as very individual and private experiences, but when we engage in contemplative witnessing, we are opening up our most honest selves to others to allow our human dignity and belovedness to be witnessed and affirmed. We can experience contemplation communally as we extend the divine gaze to our collective and experience a mutual attentiveness to our whole. We are all witnesses to one another. We witness each other's life experiences and transformations over time. We can also accompany each other on our sacred encounters within.

A spiritual director or companion is one of my roles, but this communal practice is not limited to trained spiritual directors. *Spiritual direction* is one Western term and framework for spiritual care, but spiritual care is much bigger and there are a variety of cultural paradigms for this practice and they can take many other forms. Spiritual care includes the many communal practices of sitting with others in order to attend to the inner life that sustains the well-being of our relationships and communities. As an Asian American practitioner, I imagine myself joining a long line of community healers in my own tradition, including Eastern medicine doctors, shamans, wise elders, and spiritual teachers. Community healers also include our grandmothers, mothers, and elders who may not have had formal education and titles but who exemplified communal care through hospitality, natural remedies, and prayers.

Therefore, I use the term *contemplative witnessing* instead of *spiritual direction* in this book to recognize the many non-Western frameworks of spiritual care that may not always have the opportunity to be named and recognized. I am a spiritual director in my formal practice, but a contemplative witness is who I aspire to be in community. A witness is a way of being I can embody even as a leader, activist, or healer. I believe that for our collective healing we all need to cultivate a healing presence in ourselves in order to be a healing presence in community. In this book, then, I refer to all of us as witnesses. Contemplative witnessing offers us a communal practice of care and a BIPOC-centered framework of care.

COMMUNAL CARE

A common theme I hear as a witness, particularly as I meet with women of color, is a growing sense of isolation and loneliness. I continuously hear in individuals today a deep longing for community and belonging. Our culture of self-care and individualized spirituality, although helpful and important, has reached its limitations. Our personal healing is restricted if the community around us is broken, if our religious congregations have failed us, and we're disconnected from loving experiences of human connection. Genuine experiences of community require each person to be vulnerable and risk sharing of ourselves, but we are often guarded with others because we've been hurt. We may enter into community insecure and skeptical. We have gotten used to transactional communities where we are valued only for what we can produce and contribute. There is little precedence for authentic and genuine communities, yet we all carry a deep longing to be truly known and witnessed. Every time we meet someone new, we make a choice: Will I open myself to friendship or will I guard and hide myself? For this reason, I firmly believe all the more in the importance of developing intimate soul friendships through intentional spiritual practices like witnessing because I need them too.

The health of our interior lives and our outward experiences in community share a mutual relationship. When we engage our own inner work and healing, we cultivate a grounded, compassionate presence that we then carry into community. Christian mystic and prophet Howard Thurman wrote, "I'm secure, because I hear—I hear the sound of the genuine in myself. And having learned to listen to that, I can become quiet enough, still enough, to hear the sound of the genuine in you."[1] We need to experience our self as sacred and beloved in order to experience the sacredness in others. Our religious communities don't often teach us this practice of accessing what Thurman calls "the sound of the genuine" in ourselves. We don't learn how to notice the stirrings within our own spirit or how to recognize our own voice. Without this foundation, we continuously engage in relationships with our insecurities and bring our own unhealed wounds and reactivities into our interactions with others.

Therefore, contemplative witnessing is an intentional communal effort to cultivate how we see ourselves and others as a spiritual posture. In this book I present contemplative witnessing as one framework for how we can be in healthy relationships together. We can learn to be attentive to sacred and divine movements within us, amongst us, and around us. This sacred relationship doesn't work, however, unless we intentionally allow our most sacred and honest self to be seen and witnessed by another. Contemplative witnessing invites us to engage each relationship and conversation as an intentional spiritual practice. As witnesses we are committed to listening well in a world that doesn't teach us how to listen. Listening to others without our own insecurities and reactivities getting in the way takes inner cultivation. It's a gift that not everyone is able to provide. If this way of relationship was the norm in how we experienced community, then perhaps we would no longer need formal spiritual direction.

BIPOC-CENTERED CARE

Although I initially wasn't planning to practice as a spiritual director, I did eventually begin meeting with directees because I noticed how challenging it can be to find a director of color. I try to reserve my limited time for people of color, and particularly women of color. But I also realized early on that I was not adequately trained to meet with those who are Black, Indigenous, and People of Color (BIPOC). As I met with BIPOC directees I was not prepared for the despair I heard in my directees because I often felt the same despair. In the United States we live in a racialized society in which white supremacy continuously expresses itself in violent rhetoric and policies. There seem to be unrelenting waves of communal grief and rage as mass shootings disproportionately affect communities of color and we continuously witness police brutality and violence against Black and brown bodies. Our human capacity for and encounters with hatred, violence, or just unkindness wearies our souls.

I wrote this book because we need more spiritual directors, healers, and leaders trained to embrace our identities as people of color and to center the experiences of BIPOC communities in our healing work. People of color need a deeply spiritual and embodied healing created by us and for us. In order for BIPOC communities to experience a liberating spirituality we need to be settled into our own bodies, experience the traditions and spiritualities of our cultures, and engage with communities that reflect our sacredness back to us. This healing work is deeply embodied, cultural, inner, and communal work. This book centers the experiences of BIPOC communities in the practice of communal care and provides inspirations for spiritual companions and other care practitioners as we facilitate healing spaces. We can embrace our roles as practitioners of color.

This book also considers how we take care of our collective spirit as we live in racist and oppressive contexts. BIPOC-centered care recognizes our collective spirituality. What is happening socially, politically, economically, and globally affects our well-being. Every chapter is about our collective wholeness because we can't heal by ourselves. We may have learned to slow down, rest, and care for our own wounds, but the world is still deeply broken, violent, and traumatic. For our healing to evolve, our next step is to pursue our communal healing. We are each part of our collective well-being, and the collective is essential to our personal well-being. Contemplative witnesses serve as healers in our communities. We have the potential to be activists that advocate for our collective care and rest. This book is written for those that seek to be healers in our broken world.

GUIDING QUESTIONS AND SACRED MOVEMENTS

The core of contemplative witnessing is asking questions that deepen or expand our everyday life experiences. There are three guiding questions I ask myself that help me center and focus my listening particularly with communities of color.

> What experience in your life needs to be witnessed in community today?
>
> How are you experiencing your most sacred, honest self?
>
> What does communal healing and restoration look like?

These three questions make up the main sections of this book: contemplative witnessing, sacred movements, and our collective spirit. I begin with the foundational elements of contemplative witnessing. Then, as I'm listening to others, I particularly listen for sacred movements that underly every experience and story. On the surface, someone may be telling a story about work or a relationship, but I am listening for movements underneath the surface. These sacred movements are not just internal but also embodied and divine movements. The sacred movements in this book include cultivating spaciousness, accessing our sources, cyclical healing, and decolonizing spirituality. These movements are not prescriptive or linear. They are also not to be forced onto others. Instead, we are witnesses to these movements as they happen. We pay attention to these movements in someone else, but we also notice them in ourselves. I then end the book by looking at how we may care for our collective spirit through our communal attunements. We also have collective sacred movements. Two collective movements discussed in this book are generational healing and restoring harmony.

I often use guided meditative practices to lean into these movements. With each of the six sacred movements in the book I begin with a guided practice that I may use with others or even for myself. Because the stories I've witnessed as a spiritual director are kept confidential, I don't share the stories of my directees in this book as examples. Instead, I will share my own stories of the sacred movements I've experienced over the years. Writing this book is a practice for myself to share my sacred self with you. Thank you for companioning and witnessing me through this book.

—

Contemplative Witnessing

What experience in your life needs to be witnessed in community today?

In our current times, most of us have experienced how social media has brought to light social injustices that have been happening all along. The difference now is technology allows us to more readily see. We live in times in which we are made intentional and unintentional witnesses of national and global events. Whether mass casualties, natural disasters, unjust killings, genocides, or corporate and political misdeeds, we can witness these injustices and tragedies in real time, up close, and on a viral scale. To be a witness gives us power as well as responsibility because each time we are a witness we must decide how we respond to what we see and hear.

Social media brought a new iteration of vicarious trauma, and witnessing can become overwhelming and exhausting as social media allows for us to be constantly aware of peoples' sufferings. We are currently testing our human capacity as witnesses of hatred and violence. We are experiencing how witnessing affects the health of our bodies, minds, and spirits.

Our tendency in response to the onslaught of potentially traumatic news can be to numb ourselves. We become more desensitized the more that we witness brutality and death. We fill our lives with distractions so that we don't have to confront the anxieties, fears, and weariness in our spirits or in our collective spirit. The more we numb ourselves and turn away from human suffering, though, the more inhumane we become. Korean Christian scholar-activist and Buddhist dharma teacher Chung Hyun Kyung wrote in *Struggle to Be the Sun Again*, "Numbing oneself for survival is the most tragic stage for the oppressed because the individual loses the power to resist."[1] As human beings we are made to be in community and to be attuned to each other. Constant turning away and numbing forms calloused hearts. We disconnect ourselves from the human responses of empathy, compassion, and kindness. For this reason, we need a spiritual posture to be more intentional in how we are witnesses.

Contemplative witnessing is a way to stay attentive to our humanity. It is a practice to cultivate seeing the divine in others, especially when institutional, political, and economic powers don't often acknowledge the human dignity in people. Witnessing requires a mutual attentiveness to our own care as well as attending to the community. For those of us that desire to be healers and activists, contemplative witnessing is an intentional spiritual posture we cultivate to be a healing presence in the world.

When I sit with people of color, I first listen for what they need me to witness in their lives. We are witnesses of the social injustices, wrongs, griefs, and pains we experience in a Western-dominated culture. When people of color come to us to be witnessed, questions we can ask ourselves are: What do they experience in our presence? Do they experience rest and restoration? Do they experience their sacredness? Do they experience freedom? Facilitating spaces of care must be qualitatively different from the day-to-day oppressive spaces we navigate through. The following five practices can help facilitate a rhythm of contemplative witnessing through listening together, speaking our truths, communal silence, communal response, and cultivating presence.

Listening Together

Contemplative witnessing begins with a communal listening together for what we need our community to witness in us. Sometimes this listening is facilitated with a moment of shared silence or a guided practice. In this shared listening, a contemplative witness intentionally shifts our attentiveness to another. We can listen not only to ourselves, but we can listen with and for others. The role of the witness is to invite us into a deeper listening of our lives. Witnessing is not simply good conversations. In contemplative witnessing there is a quality of conversation that comes out of our listening and out of the depths of our most honest selves.

As I train spiritual directors, one of the common challenges my students struggle with is how to gently stop people who speak incessantly. They are afraid of being rude, but sometimes it's a gift to gently stop someone. As we listen, we carefully discern where one's speaking is coming from. When we speak from a space of mental processing and reasoning, from a defensive stance, or just a vomiting of everything going on in life, we are not actually speaking from our listening. A gift we can offer as witnesses is to invite each other to pause, take a step back from our indiscriminate talking, and instead invite one another to access the deepest parts of ourselves, and to listen for our most honest, sacred selves. When we begin with this shared listening perhaps we discover that what needs to be witnessed is something we ourselves aren't aware of yet. We may have internalized experiences that need to emerge from deep within ourselves.

Speaking Our Truths

Contemplative witnessing invites us into the brave act of speaking our truths, stories, and experiences. Speaking our truths moves us out of our isolation and disconnection and is how we connect to community. By speaking out our truths, we are giving the community the opportunity to witness us and for our sacred self to be known. We all have experiences in which we need another human being to know what happened. We don't necessarily need others to offer a solution. We just need someone else to hear our side of the story, acknowledge what we experienced, and believe that it happened. The life experiences that we need witnessed by community are many. Sometimes we have challenging experiences in which we felt dismissed or harmed. We also have seasons of grief, anger, pain, or all those emotions at once.

Furthermore, BIPOC communities may regularly have race-related interactions that include gaslighting, microaggressions, entitlement, and dismissing, in addition to more overt racist remarks and actions. Sometimes racism is experienced through offhand comments masked in niceness, in gaslighting where we are made to question ourselves, or through navigating institutional systems with invisible barriers. These occurrences happen so often that by now we're not necessarily surprised by them and we know how to get through them. We can become so used to these experiences that we often push them down, ignore them, and move on in order to survive and keep going with our lives.

But these moments, big and small, build up in us over time. Sometimes we just need someone to hear, someone to be a witness of what we experience. Sometimes we need a witness because in our own minds we may second-guess and question ourselves. We may wonder if we're being too sensitive, overanalyzing, or perhaps misunderstood intentions. So we need witnesses in community so that we might trust our intuitions and have others reflect back to us the reality of what we experienced. Being witnessed in community helps us acknowledge and attend to the ways we are hurt or dismissed.

There also doesn't need to be a problem to be witnessed. We equally need to share our accomplishments with each other and allow the community to celebrate us. We also need to notice the ways in which we're changing and evolving in each season of life. We need to speak out the special moments in which we're really proud of ourselves and who we're becoming. Sometimes we need to share our mystical or supernatural encounters that are beyond the norm of everyday occurrences. We might keep these experiences to ourselves for fear of being rejected. Being witnessed helps us to see the significance of our accomplishments, experiences, and transformations. As communal beings all these life experiences need to be witnessed in community.

Speaking as a contemplative practice is the spiritual act of naming. We may have developed a lifelong pattern of suppressing our most honest emotions and responses. Speaking it out may be an active choice we need to make to unform our habit of suppressing. Especially for BIPOC communities, speaking our truths in our own words gives us agency over our own narratives. We can speak our stories in the reality in which we experienced them. By speaking our truths, we allow the community to witness our humanity, to affirm our sacredness, and to restore our dignity. Rather than constantly pushing down our emotions and physical reactions, there is healing in speaking it out.

Communal Silence and Response

In contemplative witnessing a communal silence is a way of honoring what was spoken. This is a thick and tangible silence that affirms what was heard and surrounds the one being witnessed. In this communal silence we witness through our felt presence. We can continue listening to one another, not through words, but through a shared connection. Silence, however, is not the end. In the communal silence witnesses attune to our own internal reactions and responses in order to discern what is our own to keep and what is a response or question that may be offered to the ones we witness.

Whenever we serve as witness for another human being, this act of witnessing is then followed by a choice. We must ask: What do we do with what we've seen or heard? The truths we witness are not up for debate or critique; however, they do need to be acknowledged. Witnessing is not just listening; it is also believing what is spoken. Healing comes from being heard and believed. The term *witnessing* is reminiscent of the Black church tradition in which witnessing is a practice of communal healing that invites an entire congregation, for example, to actively engage with each other's stories of sufferings, pains, and injustices. The congregation affirms the presence of God and the community as sources of care and strength even in the suffering. Witnessing invites the congregation to be present to one another's experiences through verbal, embodied, and communal affirmations.

A Western-centric contemplative movement has allowed the value of silence to overrule issues of injustice and harm. Traditionally, Western paradigms of spiritual direction train spiritual directors to remain neutral, to be silent, and to not have strong reactions or facial expressions. But silence communicates. If we are witnesses to an injustice, remaining neutral communicates complicity. As a contemplative witness we may offer the freedom of a nonjudgmental space, but that is not to be mistaken as a neutral space. We are not neutral, because we are against harm and for liberation. Contemplative witnessing is ultimately about facilitating a space to engage with our internal, embodied, and collective healing. Therefore, we are committed to facilitating spaces that are restorative.

I once shared with a small group of women an incident I experienced as a professor with a white male student who challenged, in entitled ways, any critique I gave. I presume that he wouldn't dare act with a white male professor the way that he acted around me. I was the only person of color in this small group and after sharing my experiences the group seemed to skip over what I so vulnerably offered and the conversation moved on. Later on they each shared with me how they felt self-conscious of their whiteness as I spoke. They didn't want to say the wrong thing, so they chose to say nothing at all. They centered their own discomfort rather than my experience. I reflected with them that when I shared this experience with women of color they didn't remain silent. They named the injustices and called out the harm as witnesses to my story.

In contemplative witnessing, we do not use silence to be complicit to harm or violence. When we believe that something is an injustice, then the next step is to call it out and name it. We need to name when human dignity is dismissed and when there is harm. We should leave no doubt or question in the minds of those speaking their story. Oftentimes, just having someone else name the harms we've experienced brings us into a deeper layer of attunement to how we're affected by the harm. There is power in having someone else reflect our truths back to us. Because of the harm of silence that I've experienced in Western-centered contemplative groups, I have reframed group spiritual direction and contemplative groups with this witnessing framework.

Those we witness may be navigating their day-to-day lives in patriarchal systems, homophobic systems, racist systems, ableist systems, and other oppressive contexts. These systems deny our sacredness and distort our humanity. BIPOC communities especially need witnesses who believe our everyday experiences of injustice in these systems which tend to deny any experiences that are outliers to the dominant norm. When we are dismissed or rejected by harmful communities, contemplative witnessing is an act that can restore us into welcoming and affirming communities.

Cultivating Presence

Contemplative witnessing is ultimately a presence we cultivate in ourselves wherever we may be. I hope that the presence I offer as a spiritual director is who I am no matter who I'm with. In the book *Casting Indra's Net*, Buddhist pastoral counselor Pamela Ayo Yetunde wrote, "Although we can never know for certain in advance that our witnessing will be helpful, I believe a contemplative lifestyle lays the groundwork for improving our intuition in this regard."[2] The challenge in becoming a contemplative witness is that it's not about learning good listening skills. Cultivating a contemplative presence requires us to first engage our own inner work and healing, and that's what makes this communal practice so difficult. We need to be a listening presence for ourselves and attuned to our own inner movements to be an open listening presence for someone else. We equally need to be witnessed by our community, even as we serve as witnesses to others.

Western-based spiritual-direction relationships can feel restrictive and imbalanced. My directees share with me the most vulnerable parts of themselves and speak of experiences that they might not tell anyone else. Yet, they barely know anything about me. This knowledge gives me power in the relationship as I hold their stories and vulnerabilities, while my directees don't have the same power over me. Thus, I continue to reflect on ways I can share my vulnerabilities with my directees and also empower them in our relationship.

It's only come with longevity, however, as I've known some of my directees for several years, that I suddenly noticed one day that my directees do know me well. They know me by my presence. I'm not used to this way of being known. In our relationship, it doesn't matter that they don't know my accomplishments or life experiences or that I've written books. But they become very familiar with my cadence, my rhythm, my silences, and my voice. They are very comfortable with how I show up and how they feel around me. This realization invited me to be more intentional about the presence I cultivate and the presence I bring into community. Today, I long to be known by my presence more than anything else.

As witnesses we can ask ourselves, what is the presence that I want to be known for? Allow for words, feelings, and images to come to you. Notice what that presence feels like in your body. Then check in with yourself routinely. In what ways have you continued to cultivate and embody that presence in your everyday interactions?

Sacred Movements

How are you experiencing your most sacred, honest self?

Whenever we enter a conversation, we often begin by talking about events. We share what's happening in our lives—the frustrating thing that happened at work, the adorable things our kids did, or the new restaurant we tried. Oftentimes conversations don't move beyond our updates of recent life events. When we feel lonely despite being around people it can be because our conversations remain at this initial layer and our sacred selves don't have a chance to be expressed or known in community. As contemplative witnesses, however, we are listening for deeper layers—for the sacred movements underneath our life events.

Whenever I start a session with a directee they too begin by telling me about recent occurrences in their life. The two most common topics my directees bring into spiritual direction are work and relationships. Our spirituality can be found in the midst of the everyday routines and dynamics of life. As a witness I may respond to what is shared by mirroring back what I heard, or noticing and naming what was spoken. At the same time, I am also listening for the layers that lie beneath the experience. I ask questions to help the one speaking to also access the layers beneath their story. Underlying every event are our reactions, such as our emotional and physical responses. As a witness, I may ask simple attunement questions like "How did you feel?" or "What did you notice in your body?" As human beings we also engage in meaning-making. We attach significance and interpretations to everything we experience. To aid in this meaning-making I may ask questions about the connections, importance, understandings, or implications of their experiences. Meaning-making, however, is often still a process of the mind. Underneath our initial responses and processing is another layer—the sacred movements.

Paying attention to sacred movements is what distinguishes contemplative witnessing from our everyday conversations. Sacred movements are the ways we express and experience our sacred self through each season of life. A contemplative witness helps us notice and attend to our selves. We might ask questions about the ways we're deepening, evolving, or expanding. We might also make connections between our experiences with divine presence and divine invitations. Through sacred movements we access our deepest longings and desires. Our imaginative and dream spaces are also sacred movements as these are movements that allow our sacred self to expand beyond our current and physical limitations. Contemplative witnesses invite us to honor and center our sacred self and to embrace our sacred movements. They slowly guide us to engage with deeper and deeper layers.

Each time we enter into a contemplative witnessing relationship we are intentionally opening up our attunements to these sacred movements. Witnessing is not just asking good questions and facilitating meaningful conversations, it is intentional listening for what is sacred that is happening in another person and in the stories they tell. We ask deepening questions in order to invite the unnoticed or unspoken parts of ourselves to come into awareness. We witness the transformations in how each of us is coming to a greater knowing, expanding, or experiencing of our full selves.

I use the term *movement* to imply flow. Movements can change, adapt, and shift. As witnesses we hold no expectations for where a sacred movement will guide us or how one's healing and restoration might happen, but we pay attention and allow the sacred to slowly evolve and reveal itself. Both the witness and the one being witnessed may be surprised by what emerges. Movements can't always be explained, instead they are primarily experienced. In Daoist spirituality these movements are thought of as energies that we can sense and cultivate. For those that believe in God or Creator, these movements are the dynamic interactions of a divine Spirit with our everyday lives.

I believe that each ethnic or cultural community also has sacred movements that are unique to our own peoples. Traditionally, wisdom teachers, shamans, and healers are those known to be especially connected to the sacred movements in our communities. Our cultural movements ask us to envision how our own people can access our sacredness and how our own people experience liberation. In my own Taiwanese heritage, for example, a sacred movement for our communal liberation is to unform the harm caused by a strong Confucian patriarchy that has suppressed and violated women for centuries. At the same time, a Daoist spirituality that believes in the feminine energy of the Dao, divine presence, can be a healing movement to uproot the patriarchy in our families and societies. A cultural sacred movement, then, is not necessarily a complete rejection of our culture. Instead, we can find healing resources from within our cultural traditions. Each ethnic and cultural group can access and determine their own liberation, often times by listening to the prophetic voices and movements on the margins of our societies.

The term *movement* is also associated with our bodies. We can pay attention to how our bodies communicate and express sacred movements. We can also physically engage sacred movements through practices like yoga, tai chi, or dance, where each body posture, rhythm, or action holds a particular intention. Whereas Western societies may perceive these as exercises, in many non-Western cultures these movements are spiritual and supernatural. The movements can be thresholds that carry our physical bodies into the spiritual realm. Whenever we learn a new embodied practice, we pay attention to our postures and also where our bodies resist movement. After much practice, however, our bodies can naturally flow in the movements without thinking, we then follow the natural guidance of our bodies. Our embodied movements can open up our internal sacred movements. And, vice versa, our inner movements can help reconnect us to our physical being as sacred in areas where we may have disassociated from our bodies.

Navigating Resistances

Our sacred selves are constantly expressing themselves. But in the busyness of life we are often disconnected from and unaware of the sacred movements that surround us and move within us. For BIPOC communities, our sacred selves may be neglected as we navigate through institutions that don't welcome our truest selves. Accessing our sacred self, then, often requires navigating through built-up layers of avoidances and resistances. Healing is hard work because we all have developed inner resistances.

Oftentimes our resistance to silence, slowing down, rest, and solitude isn't a resistance to the silence and stillness itself, but a resistance to confronting our honest selves. Silence is a mirror that reveals the state of our souls. Our bodies may physically resist as we fidget, and our minds resist by suddenly dwelling on our unfinished to-do list. Thus, when we express our most sacred selves in community, it can feel raw and vulnerable, especially if we have not learned to love the person we encounter. So our minds and bodies will suddenly become reactive and look for distractions. When we're afraid to go within or don't know how, then sometimes we need a compassionate companion, a witness, to go with us. Contemplative witnesses facilitate such a space for journeying within and they serve as companions as we encounter our most sacred and honest selves.

One of our most common resistances is to turn to the mind. We dwell on reasonings and rationalizations. In seasons of stress our mental processing can become hyperactive as we lose sleep and experience increased anxiety as thoughts churn in our minds repeatedly. We look for answers and solutions in order to avoid the harder work of acknowledging how we feel. Our mental processing may be trying to avoid the more challenging emotions that lie underneath, such as disappointment, anger, hurt, or grief. When my directees ask for homework or helpful readings that can also be a resistance behavior to use an action as a solution instead of continuing to face their honest selves. We would prefer to read a book about healing to avoid actual healing. A contemplative witness can invite us into rest by simply asking us to take a step back from our constant mental processing.

For those that were raised in religious institutions we may be used to having authority figures prescribe our movements for us and set expectations for the ways in which we should grow, change, or behave. A resistance I notice often in Asian communities, or high power-distance cultures, is looking to a religious authority figure, even a spiritual director, as an expert. We expect the professional or authority figure to give the answers in order to avoid having to access our own knowings or having the heavy responsibility of making our own decisions.

We may also have ingrained survival mechanisms that are resistance behaviors. Survival mechanisms are the methods we've formed in order to survive oppression, trauma, and other challenges we encounter in life. We learned ways to immediately self-soothe and self-comfort to move on in life. But our survival mechanisms can also be ways of suppressing ourselves and become resistances that prevent us from engaging the deeper experiences of encountering our selves. A common survival mechanism that I especially notice in women of color is the *shoulds*. We say phrases like "I *should* trust God more" or "I *should* rest more." *Shoulds* often come out of guilt, obligation, or perfectionism. *Shoulds* can also be a survival technique to help us tolerate injustice and pains. It's a way to blame ourselves and set higher expectations for a theoretical future. As contemplative witnesses we avoid going into the should conversations with those we witness.

We cannot simply dismiss our survival mechanisms, however; instead we must honor them. Our resistances are simply trying to protect us. They are not enemies but friends that we need to compassionately attend to. To honor our survival mechanisms and resistances we might say a simple, "thank you for helping me survive" or "thank you for protecting me." We might also care for our survival mechanisms by recognizing when those mechanisms are no longer needed, and that they are free to be released now.

Moving Toward Freedom

Ultimately, sacred movements, especially for BIPOC communities, are where we experience freedom and liberation. In the last several years, as I met with my own spiritual director, our conversations have too often been a space of grief and anger with each wave of police brutality against Black and brown bodies and each tragedy of mass shootings and global violence. During the early years of the COVID-19 pandemic, however, when in the United States we saw an increase of violent attacks against Asian American elderly and witnessed shootings in Asian American communities, I observed my own voicelessness. I could notice the fears I carried in my body and how I was more self-conscious and aware of my surroundings whenever I went out, but I didn't have the words to express lament and rage for myself or my own communities. I realized then that it is easier for me to advocate for Black, Indigenous, and Latine communities than to advocate for Asian communities because that meant advocating for myself. I noticed my lifelong pattern of joining multiethnic and BIPOC communities, but avoiding solely Asian American social groups because I was avoiding a sense of inferiority in myself. This noticing with my spiritual director invited me into a deeper sacred movement that I wasn't aware of previously. I needed to address the fears that I had repressed all my life.

Although I believe it's essential for our communal liberation to advocate with and for communities different than our own, in these circumstances I can easily depersonalize my activism. My activism could be outward actions, protests, and statements, without actually coming from my own internal liberation. Advocating for Asian American communities, however, requires that I confront the ways in which I don't see my own sacredness and the ways in which I had internalized oppression in my own body. Working toward our freedom and justice is not just outward actions of protest and resistance, but actually requires deep inner work and healing. Buddhist minister Lama Rod Owens writes in the book *Radical Dharma*, "We can have this rhetoric of overthrowing oppressive systems, but we have to balance that with the work of overthrowing the oppressive system operating internally that actually keeps us enslaved."[1] For this reason, spaces for contemplative witnessing are necessary to support this hard work of healing. We each need to recognize and embrace our own bodies, social locations, and cultural experiences whatever our unique stories may be. Continual attentiveness to our sacred self is what informs and sustains our activism.

Contemplative witnessing invites us into the deep inner work we need to engage, not just as a personal commitment but in the context of community. We need to engage our sacred movements together and not in isolation. We need to be in communities that help us access the deepest layers of our experiences. We need people that ask us questions and invite us into these layers. We need community that witness our self-discoveries, the expansions of our spiritualities, and our mystical, divine connections. Community are the people that see our sacredness and remind us. In the process of recognizing what is sacred in us we also clear out what denies our sacredness. We need witnesses for all these movements of our soul.

The following sections examine a few of the sacred movements I've personally experienced, as well as witnessed with communities of color. These movements don't happen in steps and stages. There is no prescription or method. There is no expectation for how long each sacred movement takes. I also believe that in a world of an infinite divine presence, that also means there are infinite possible sacred movements. I can only name here a few. Every sacred movement, though, requires that we're able to honestly look within in self-awareness and communal awareness. We let the sacred guide us through gentle nudges and invitations. As witnesses for one another we can also play an important communal role by encouraging each other to bravely enter into these movements.

CULTIVATING SPACIOUSNESS

Practice:

Begin by taking a few deep and slow breaths. Then enter into your imagination and immerse in this origin story from ancient Daoist philosophers and adapted from theologian Grace Ji-Sun Kim's *The Holy Spirit, Chi, and the Other.*

In the beginning, there was *chi* 氣 (which in Chinese means sacred breath and sacred spirit) and *chi* existed in the beginning without form in a great void. Then this *chi*, this sacred breath, began to contract between *yin* and *yang*, dark and light. The contractions grew stronger as the sacred breath moved in and out, and then out of the *chi* emerged heaven and earth, and this *chi* continues to this day to sustain the sacred life force in all beings and in all nature and in you.[2]

Imagine yourself in this beginning. Walk around to notice what you see, hear, and touch.

Continue to breathe deeply and slowly, in and out. This is *chi.* Your sacred breath is the same as the divine and ancient breath. Your sacred breathing is the same spirit, the same *chi*, that is the life-giving force shared by all community and all our nature kin.

In Japanese there is a term called *ma* 間. This is an artistic term that refers to the empty spaces in between. If you've seen traditional Japanese paintings, you might notice that there tends to be ample spaciousness in their art. Japanese artists believe that the empty space in between is itself a valued aesthetic. Even those who cultivate bonsai trees pay attention to *ma* in the space between the branches and around the trees. *Ma* is found not only in visual art but also in the quiet lingering moments we take to listen to the rain or when we slow down our walk to notice the wind rustling through the trees. Architects and interior designers can also build the experience of *ma* by designing open space through minimalism and simplicity.

Contemplative witnesses too are cultivators of the space in between. The space in contemplative witnessing is the presence held between people. We pay attention to the space in between words or what's left unsaid. We take intentional pauses and invite listening to expand the space in a conversation. When someone enters the presence of a contemplative witness there is often a felt, tangible shift. The witness carries a certain presence that invites us to slow down, to rest, and to be attentive as a way to open up spaciousness in the midst of our often full lives.

Spaciousness is especially important for BIPOC communities that may have lived in constant survival mode. Therese Taylor-Stinson and Paula Owens Parker, founding members of the Spiritual Directors of Color Network, write in the book *Kaleidoscope*, "Until survival is not the pressing issue, there is no psyche space for reexamination and self-awareness."[3] We need financial security, a sense of safety, rest, and other basic needs met in order to experience spaciousness. Rest is a justice issue. If people in our communities don't have access to rest, then they don't have the spaciousness to access their creativities and imaginations. We need spaciousness to imagine a different way of being and to creatively live into our liberation. Spaciousness may feel like a luxury, especially if we had immigrant or working-class parents and grandparents that made tremendous sacrifices for our family's livelihood. Even in their old age our elders may not have known how to stop their busy movements as their minds and bodies got used to constant productivity and work their whole lives. But spaciousness and rest are not privileged experiences, they are human rights. Spaciousness can be a foundational sacred movement for our generational healing as we can slow down and rest for our elders and ancestors who could not. Spaciousness and rest cannot be attained alone. In our society of unequal rest, we need a communal effort to create spaciousness for one another. We need an active collective resistance to the constant productivity of a capitalist system.

As witnesses we can offer the gift of spaciousness. We create a space that invites one another to relax our bodies and slow down our propensity toward constant activity. We can offer this gift both in formal practice as well as through the presence we carry in community. If the first thing that a directee says to me is how busy they are in this season, then I consider how the space and time we share together can be a place of rest. We don't discuss theoretical plans like how they could make more time for rest or plan for more self-care. Instead of putting off our rest into the future or scheduling it on our calendar, we slow down now and we rest in the present, because that's what our shared practice together is for.

Women of color especially operate with unrealistic high expectations of ourselves. We have been expected to perform at 150% in order to prove ourselves in systems and institutions not made for us. We then may internalize these high expectations and hold ourselves to perfection. As a witness I may invite women of color to the spaciousness of not needing to prove ourselves to other people. Contemplative witnessing can offer rest from our everyday weariness of navigating systems not made for us.

Chinese Daoist philosopher Chuang Tzu wrote, "Everybody knows the use of usefulness, but nobody seems to know the use of uselessness."[4] Oftentimes in our culture of productivity we feel we must accomplish something even in our rest, that our rest must be productive too, filled with practices and goals. If all that happens in contemplative witnessing is a pause, a slowing down, and open space, then that's enough. We are not using spiritual practices to help each other tolerate oppressive conditions and impossible expectations, but instead our work as witnesses is to fiercely protect each other's rest and spaciousness under oppressive conditions.

If spaciousness can be a presence that we carry, then as contemplative witnesses we can intentionally cultivate this spaciousness. A question I ask myself daily is "Do I have space in myself today to be present to another human being?" If I have directees for the day or if I plan to be in community, then I check in with myself. If I don't have space in myself, I can cause harm to the community through inattentiveness, impatience, or reactivity. There are many simple practices we can do to open up our spaciousness. We can immerse ourselves in wide open spaces in nature or take a long walk after a heavy conversation. We might spend a day with no plans or agenda. We can engage in physical or artistic activities that help us access the nonverbal parts of our brain. We can set aside a time from as brief as two minutes to as long as an indefinite season, with spaciousness as the only intention. We allow ourselves to daydream, to clear out, and to breathe. The more space we cultivate in ourselves the more space we can offer to those around us.

Facilitating spaciousness in a relationship is an art form. Spaciousness can be cultivated in conversations through the intentions of breath, slow, and pause. We use embodied spaciousness to cultivate a spacious presence and to invite those we witness into their spaciousness.

Breath

These days there are many scientific research articles about the physical and mental health benefits of breath practices, especially for regulating our bodies and emotions, but we didn't actually need modern science to tell us this. There are many ancient traditions that have known the power of breath for many centuries, including the Yogic tradition as well as the Daoist tradition, through practices like tai chi and qi gong. In these ancient traditions, breath is both physical and mystical. These traditions hold a worldview that doesn't separate or distinguish the physical from the supernatural. The sacred movement of breath can be found in the Sanskrit term *prana*, in the Chinese *qi* or *chi*, *ki* in Japanese, or *ruach* in Hebrew. These terms don't have direct English translations because they simultaneously mean breath, spirit, and life-force. Our breath can move us into the spirit realm and the spirit realm can flow through us through our physical breath. Breath is a practice of embodied spaciousness that also facilitates our inner spaciousness. Our sacred breath is also shared with the divine breath, as well as shared with the life-force in all of nature. Therefore, breath is a simple yet sacred spiritual practice that we can also experience as a synchronous communal practice to open up our attunements and our physical, mental, emotional, and spiritual capacities.

Slow

In our everyday conversations we often operate in a mode of quick back-and-forth dialogue. Sometimes our propensity toward debate and critique in our everyday discourse is harsh on our spirits as it requires us to defend our ideas. Contemplative witnessing invites us into experiencing a slow and gentle conversation. We intentionally slow down our pace. We patiently wait and allow what needs to be witnessed to arise and emerge from deep within us. We invite attentiveness to our internal movements, sometimes through meditative and embodied practices. We wait and listen for however long is needed for the sacred to arise in us. We never hurry our conversation or our experiences. Slow gives each word, feeling, or sensation weight and importance. For those unaccustomed to slowing down, we gently invite each other to ease in by slowing down our breath, our activity, and the constant churning of our minds. Slow allows for our inner work and healing to go deeper rather than to remain at the surface.

To intentionally cultivate a slowing down in my own life I spent a year in intentional slowness. I started with embodied slowness. I slowed down my breathing, walking, eating, and other movements. I used Vietnamese Zen master Thich Nhat Hanh's series of books on *How to See*, *How to Eat*, *How to Walk*, and *How to Sit* as meditations for mindful physical movements.[5] Of course, as I attempted to slow down I gained a heightened awareness of just how often I hurry, but with graciousness I would simply remind myself to slow down again. I noticed that when I walk fast my upper body leans forward trying to get to my destination. When I slow down, my upper body relaxes and moves upright. I become present to the walk rather than the destination. I noticed that when I talk fast, I'm feeling insecure and trying to prove myself. When I talk slower, I'm more attentive and thoughtful in what I say. The embodied practices became reminders then for me to engage the rest of my life with slowness. I was slower in my reactions and responses, slower in conversations, and slower in making decisions. In reality, very few decisions in our everyday life need to be made immediately, even if our bodies and minds sense an urgency. A gift we can give to ourselves and others is to step back from urgency and offer the expectation of slow as opposed to the expectation that we need to figure out answers and solutions right away. A witness invites an intentional slowing down to linger in the pauses, ask questions to expand our spaciousness, and notice movements or shifts within us.

Pause

A contemplative witness creates in conversation a rhythm of sacred pauses and silences. Pauses help us attune to one another's emotions and felt responses as we listen to one another. Through the silence I can better connect to your joys and pains. Pausing allows those emotions space to become full. Sometimes we experience a holy communal pause when we are struck by awe by what was spoken. Often our pauses and silences invite others to share what they might otherwise not feel inclined to voice.

I was a very quiet child, which seemed to give my grandma the spaciousness to tell her stories. Whenever my paternal grandma, *ahma* in Taiwanese, was cooking, folding laundry, or giving me a bath, she would fill the silence with her life stories or stories about my father, aunts, and uncles. I remember these stories as being slow and gentle, as my silence invited *ahma* to reminisce about her life. I feel honored today as I have the privilege of carrying my grandmothers' stories. The same is true in contemplative witnessing. When we let the silence linger for even a few more uncomfortable seconds, it invites those speaking to share what may be just underneath the surface that they normally wouldn't speak. The silence somehow invites us to take a risk. Sometimes when we quiet and wait long enough there emerges from deep within us words that need to be spoken and witnessed that we weren't aware of before.

At the same time, for those with unprocessed trauma, silent pauses can be triggering. Our whole bodies may be agitated by the silence. Thus, contemplative witnesses are attentive and compassionate with what we may not be ready for. We honor limitations and boundaries. We always give others and ourselves the choice to stop or to go gently. We never force someone to be vulnerable or honest. We give those we listen to the agency and power in the conversation to determine their own comfort level and sense of safety.

Thus, our sacred pauses can also be experienced through music, art, rituals, or embodied movements. As theologian and spiritual teacher Barbara Holmes writes in *Joy Unspeakable* of the Black church tradition, "In this ethnic context, the word *contemplation* includes but does not require silence or solitude. Instead, contemplative practices can be identified in public prayers, meditative dance movements, and musical cues that move the entire congregation toward a communal listening and entry into communion with a living God."[6] Whenever I facilitate retreats I also give everyone permission to fall asleep, even while I'm talking. Sleep is a spiritual practice too. When our trauma responses are activated, then sleep is one way that our bodies protect us and how we care for ourselves. When I give the community permission to fall asleep, then at the end of the retreat people feel proud and delighted whenever they share that they took a good nap during our time together.

ACCESSING OUR SOURCES

Practice:

Daoist philosopher Chuang Tzu told the following parable that depicts a fictional conversation between Confucius, the spiritual guide, and his student. They discuss a spiritual practice called "fasting of the mind."

"'Tell me,' said the student, 'what is fasting of the mind?' Confucius replied: 'The goal of fasting is inner unity. This means hearing, but not with the ear; hearing, but not with the understanding; hearing with the spirit, with your whole being. The hearing that is only in the ears is one thing. The hearing of the understanding is another. But the hearing of the spirit is not limited to any one faculty, to the ear, or to the mind. Hence it demands the emptiness of all the faculties. And when the faculties are empty, then the whole being listens.'"[7]

This listening practice from Chuang Tzu to listen with our *chi* or spirit asks us to locate where and how we access our listening. Take a moment to notice: Do you listen from your mind or from other parts of yourself?

As contemplative witnesses we join the lineage of wisdom elders and spiritual guides through this practice of listening through spirit. In the Chinese text of this parable, the term used for hearing with spirit is *chi* 氣, the term discussed earlier as simultaneously meaning spirit, breath, and life-force.

This is the same *chi* that existed since the beginning of life. Listening with *chi* implies that listening is both embodied and mystical. We can listen in tune with the greater divine spirit. Listening with *chi* also requires connecting with the life-giving energy in all of community, including our nature community. Listening with our spirit requires first releasing the dominant ways we've been taught to listen through our minds. Instead, listening with our full selves is a felt sense that requires that we can access all our resources to listen. When we listen through our full presence, we can notice what's not spoken. We can hear feelings and desires. It is this deep inner and whole body listening that distinguishes contemplative witnessing as an intentional spiritual practice of communal listening.

We live in a modern society in which we often don't know how to listen with our whole selves. Western and patriarchal systems have valued authority and academic education as our primary sources of knowing. In this way those with power regularly take our agency. We are used to having others set standards for us of what we're supposed to think and how we're supposed to behave. These standards, however, tend to be Western and male centric. This imbalance of knowing inhibited and stunted our abilities to access our own agency and our own knowings. Over time we may realize that we no longer know how to access our own voice, our own sources, our cultural wisdoms, or our divine connections. One of the most powerful sacred movements of contemplative witnessing is learning to access our own inherent sources, which includes our own connections to and experiences of the divine.

A contemplative witness gives agency by not forcing our own knowledge over others. Rather we give agency by guiding others in how to access their own listening. This may be a kind of relationship we're not used to. If a contemplative witness does not claim our own knowings over others, then we release our needs to problem solve, fix, or give advice. As witnesses we fully believe that every person has their own agency, their own resources, knowings, and divine connections to come to their own resolutions. When we don't attempt to bring a resolution, we are believing in the full agency of the one we witness to come to their own resolutions in their own time. If we respond with our own solutions, we may be cutting off the opportunity of the one we witness to access their most sacred selves.

Contemplative witnesses are attuned to our own listening sources while facilitating a space for others to attune to theirs. As witnesses we are not suppressing ourselves as we listen. Instead, we are very attuned to ourselves, our own responses, and our own experiences and stories. Although we may not always speak our experiences and stories, we are accessing our sources and experiences to inform how we listen and how we form questions. The hardest part about training new spiritual directors or contemplative witnesses is that the training is ultimately not about skills, but about inner awareness into our own mental chatter and emotional responses. A witness learns to be attentive and responsible for our own self-attunement in order to not cause harm to a relationship with reactionary responses or centering oneself in someone else's story. Contemplative witnessing as a way of being in nonharmful relationships is a way intentionally cultivated. We may need to retrain our mental, emotional, and physical responses to give ample space and time for others to access their own sources and to release our own discomforts in wanting to fill the space with our own needs. We can cultivate this attentiveness to ourselves and others through the intentional postures of nonattachment, ways of being, and trusting our sources.

Nonattachment

Nonattachment, or detachment, is a spiritual posture found in many religious traditions, and it is the posture of a contemplative witness. In Daoist, Buddhist, and Hindu traditions this posture is found in the terms *wuwei* in Chinese or *aparigraha* in Sanskrit. This term is sometimes translated as "nonaction," but is more accurately translated as nonattachment or nonpossessiveness. This posture does not mean to not do anything. Rather, nonattachment is the opposite of a colonizing energy which has a need to control, accumulate, and dominate. Nonattachment is best cultivated in learning to live in relationship with nature by accepting nature's constant change and adapting to nature as opposed to trying to utilize, control, and manipulate nature for our own purposes.

As contemplative witnesses we can cultivate nonattachment not only in our relationship to nature, but also in our relationships with one another. Nonattachment means not forcing things to happen in someone else's life and invites us to let go of control of other people. We release the need for other people to validate us or to give us our sense of worth. Instead, we engage our own inner work to cultivate our own inherent worth gifted to us by divine presence. Forming a posture of nonattachment takes a lifetime of cultivation as our internal needs to prove ourselves will continuously emerge in different ways in our interactions with others. Nonattachment is also vital for our own well-being as witnesses as it releases us from the heavy burdens of being responsible for everyone's problems. We're able to trust each person's agency, choices, and responsibilities, as well as consequences. As a contemplative witness we must trust that everyone has their own resources and their own access to divine and sacred wisdoms.

Ways of Being

Even though in witnessing we may not tell people *what* to do, we can facilitate a *how.* The majority of people I meet with may not know how to access their own knowings or they question and doubt themselves. The most common question people of the Christian faith ask me is "How do I listen for God's voice and not my own?" But this question creates a false dichotomy. We are not listening for God's voice and neglecting our own. Instead, we are listening for where our own desires and divine intentions align. We may have trouble listening for divine spirit because we may not even know how to listen to ourselves. Our abilities to access our own sources have been constrained, thus a healing movement a witness might facilitate is to open up pathways to reconnect and attune to ourselves again and to our whole being. When someone asks me a question, even if I have an answer, I can choose to respond with deepening questions rather than my own answers so that the one I witness can come to their own knowings. When we can come to our holy knowings on our own, it's much more powerful and lasting than someone simply telling us.

A sacred movement for BIPOC communities is to reconnect to our many cultural ways of knowing and being that we may have lost access to. Here I include the phrase "ways of being" because the word *knowing* tends to be associated with the mind. "Ways of being" reminds us that our knowings can come from internal, embodied, and communal sources.

Thus, for communities of color we not only learn how to access our cultural ways of being, but we also trust these cultural ways as just as valid and valuable as a cognitive knowing, even if the dominant culture may not recognize these alternative ways of being. We must trust that all our modes of listening, knowing, and being are how divine presence communicates with us. This is how Spirit works within us. Divine Spirit can communicate in a diversity of ways, not just through study, reasoning, and rationalizing. If we limit our interactions with God or a sacred presence to what we can cognitively process, then we limit the sacred movements in our lives. In witnessing we must trust that all our sources of listening, knowing, and being are valid sources for us to pay attention to.

There are infinite ways of being in this world, and each cultural and spiritual tradition can teach us more. But the following are just a few of the sources we have access to. Our *internal* ways of being include paying attention to our emotions, imaginations, and intuitions. These three internal ways of being are often dismissed and suppressed in our post-Enlightenment culture. Our intuitions are felt senses that we all have, but they may not conform to the logic of the dominant culture. Our imaginations speak to us in images and prophecies that may not exist yet. Thus it takes intentional practice to learn how to trust and value these internal ways again. Our *embodied* ways of being are the ways our bodies communicate to us through aches and pains, desires and pleasures. Oftentimes our bodies communicate to us before our minds can even process these physical knowings. We can also access embodied ways of knowing through our connections to nature. Nature communicates wisdom to us through our physical senses and sensations. We may also have *mystical* and *supernatural* experiences that are ways of being that don't fit into our human language or categories. Dreams are also supernatural sources. Dreams are especially the primary communication channel of our ancestors to us. Our *communal* ways of being also include ancestral wisdoms, the teachings of elders, and our cultural rituals.

Often in contemplative witnessing we are accompanying people through seasons of transition, change, or discernment. Western discernment is often presented as individual choice and calling, whereas in collective cultures discernment considers our role in the community. In the West, we may practice self-centric decision making, which also assumes everyone has the privilege of choice. This view of discernment has us constantly trying to distinguish ourselves. We are future-focused and pushing ahead. We may make decisions based on what is most practical and beneficial for ourselves. We pursue career paths, but this pushing never stops. We never feel fulfilled.

In collective cultures discernment is accessing our communal identity and resources, not just our individual desires. A contemplative witness helps us open up our attunements to our selves, our communities, and the divine to guide us. We connect with our values through our many sources of being and knowing. In individual discernment, we often ask "What do I do?" This question is action-focused and we may anxiously seek a solution based on fear of making the wrong decision. A contemplative witness can gently shift the question and ask us "Who are you to be?" This shifts the question to pay attention to our presence and relationships and not just our actions. Sometimes when we listen with our spirit instead of our minds the choices we make aren't the most rational or practical decisions, but we know they are the right decisions for our well-being and the well-being of our communities. When we can sense who we are to be, then what we are to do also becomes clearer.

An important source for all of us is our community. When we ask ourselves who are we to be, we are also accessing our role in the community. We can move beyond a self-centric way of being to a communal way of being. The community can mirror our sacredness to us and remind us of our essential place in the whole. Therefore, an important spiritual practice we can incorporate in our lives is to gather trusted friends and family each time we are in life transitions and invite each other to help us listen. This communal listening does not mean giving advice but is an invitation to listen with and for each other with a community of people that are both our witnesses and our advocates. I hope that communal discernment practices become a norm in our communities so that we intentionally call on our community as a sacred source.

Trusting Our Sources

The most difficult challenge is not simply accessing our sources, but actually trusting what we hear, notice, or know. As a witness I have noticed that we often have harmful voices in our minds that are not our own. We give power to other people's expectations of us. We are plagued by voices of self-doubt, criticism, and perfectionism. For women of color, we especially are led by our sense of obligation and self-sacrifice. These voices make us question ourselves. We then operate from our outer selves and how others perceive us, rather than an inner knowing of ourselves. As a witness, when I hear people speaking from these critical and mean voices we've internalized, questions I might ask are "Whose voice is that? Is it yours?" Only through the practice of listening can we begin to distinguish our own sacred voice from the voices that don't belong to us. This listening requires releasing the harmful voices that are not our own in order to access our own inherent knowings.

The most frequent spiritual practice I facilitate with women of color is to take time to listen to ourselves. We listen and notice without judgment or trying to fix, which may be our normal mode of operation in our families and workplaces. A misconception of meditative practices is that we need to push away and ignore all our thoughts, and if we have thoughts those are distractions. But in a full-being listening nothing is a distraction. Everything that comes to us—thoughts, emotions, physical sensations, intuitions, memories, and so on—is there for a reason. We need to learn to be attentive to all the ways that our whole selves may communicate with us. We so often stuff down and ignore these communications throughout the day that we need to intentionally invite them to come to our awareness and attend to every part of ourselves.

When these varied ways of being are affirmed and witnessed in community it helps us to trust. This is the power of community. Oftentimes in conversation we'll mention our sense of knowing as just passing comments: for example, "I had a strange dream last night" or "my stomach hurts today." My role as a witness is to intentionally turn our attention to those passing comments as wisdoms worthy of our attention. I might invite attunement by asking "Can you tell me about that dream?" or "What's going on with your stomach?" The more we pay attention to our sources of knowing and being, the more we learn to trust ourselves. One of the primary roles of the witness is to help us pay attention and listen to all our sacred knowings. On the days in which we can't access our own voice or our own sources, then we need witnesses that remind us. When we don't believe we have a voice, then our community of witnesses believes for us. When we are doubting and questioning ourselves, our community of witnesses name what is false. Witnesses trust and believe our sacredness until we can access our own sacredness again.

CYCLICAL HEALING

Practice:

Listen for a question your soul may be asking in this season.

Don't analyze what your question may be. Just wait. Allow a question to arise from within you.

When a question arises, don't answer the question.

Practice allowing the question to remain as a question.

In my first year as a spiritual director, I started to get bored. It seemed like each of my directees had an issue that came back up in our conversations again and again, if not the next month then two or three months later. The repetition made me question my own effectiveness in facilitating spiritual care. Until one day, as I met with my own spiritual director, I suddenly noticed I have the exact same pattern! I also have one or two issues in my life that keep coming back into our conversations again and again, month after month, year after year. That's when I realized that healing is cyclical.

The unhealthy patterns in our lives are also cyclical. These patterns are often ingrained protection mechanisms that will come up each time we are stressed or anxious. These unhealthy patterns may be ways we try to grasp for control when life becomes uncertain. The cyclical nature of unhealthy patterns in our lives may feel frustrating as it's very difficult to break these habits. At the same time, with each cycle we have agency and choice. We can rely on our same patterns or we can choose healing. If our unhealthy patterns are ingrained in us through repetition, then healing will also require repetition.

Cyclical healing is how our souls work things out. There's a Chinese term, *xin jie* 心結, which can be literally translated as "heart knots." Heart knots are the inner issues in our life that hinder us from our own healing and liberation. I like the imagery of heart knots as it reminds me of the continual effort it takes to pull out a difficult knot, but with each pull it may loosen just a little bit more until one day the knot gives and becomes free. The same is true for addressing the root issues that will ultimately lead to our freedom. We keep coming back to them again and again throughout our lives.

In each cycle of healing we either deepen or expand or evolve, even if slightly. Each time we return to our unhealthy patterns or root issues it may mean we're ready for the next layer or evolvement of our healing. Perhaps we return with a new perspective or a different experience. There is no time expectation for how long cyclical healing may take. Some deeply rooted issues will take a lifetime of engagement. Each layer may be unraveling a false self that we've embodied our whole lives up until now. Our areas of healing may be generational traumas and each cycle of healing is undoing historical patterns ingrained into our family dynamics. We may be engaging a cyclical movement started generations before and will continue into the generations beyond us.

We also know that divine movements are cyclical. We know this because nature models for us this cyclical transformation. We can observe cyclical patterns everywhere. Taiwanese author Derek Lin writes in his commentary on the *Tao Te Ching*, "Everything in nature exhibits a cyclical pattern: The changing seasons, the tides, the sun, the moon. All living things flourish and eventually return to their origin in the recurrent cycles of life. When we quiet the internal chatter and bear silent witness to the miraculous natural processes at work, we strengthen our connection with the empty, yet incredibly prolific creativity of the Tao."[8] *Tao* or *Dao* is the Daoist term for divine presence. If the divine presence interacts with nature in cycles, then perhaps this divine presence also interacts with humanity in cycles. Our role is to be present to these cycles, and each cycle or iteration is a sacred movement in our lives. Divine presence and nature are unhurried and unconcerned with human limitations of time. Thus, in our healing we are invited to engage with the slow, cyclical nature of transformation.

Cyclical healing incorporates our past, present, and future selves. If we don't face the past, we continue to pass on generational wounds and traumas into the future. We will perpetuate cycles of harm and pain. A liberating spirituality for BIPOC communities begins by addressing the past collectively. BIPOC communities must wrestle with the history of Western influence in our communities. We must ask how the history of colonization, slavery, colonialism, and missionary activity affect our spirituality. Oftentimes we may be asking these questions in isolation for fear of reprimand. Contemplative witnessing invites these questions into community. Wrestling with historical traumas is deeply spiritual work that is both an internal movement as well as a collective movement. We need, for our collective healing, rituals of public and communal confession and lament. Rituals are also cyclical. They are embodied movements of remembrance that expand our healing and freedom.

Holding Our Questions

The most common response in contemplative witnessing is asking deepening questions. In non-Western wisdom traditions, such as spiritual friendships in Buddhism or sage–student relationships in other traditions, the role of the spiritual guide or elder is not to give answers, but to ask good questions. Wisdom teachers are those that know what they don't know. They trust, not in their own positions of power, but that every human being can cultivate their own sacred knowings and relationships with the divine. They give us space to experience our own sacred connections. Contemplative witnesses continue these ancient traditions of spiritual friendships through asking deepening questions. Deepening questions take us into an honest place within ourselves.

Deepening questions help us attune to cyclical movements. Contemplative witnesses invite us to ask questions in order to notice and expand the movements or shifts within us. Asking deepening questions helps us to not simply move on from what we speak to the next topic, but actually linger our attention. Deepening questions help us to connect to our emotions and embodied responses that came from speaking our truths, and encourage us to explore the layers of our experiences. Through asking questions the witness enters a deeper relationship with the one we are listening to. We ask deepening questions to invite others into their own knowings and divine connections rather than our own, and we enter with them.

Contemplative witnesses are tasked with holding our questions, not simply because we ask questions, but because we're comfortable allowing questions to remain as questions. We are aware that questions need time to evolve. Questions help us to attune to cyclical movements. We offer questions without solutions because we believe that what we need most is not the answer but the transformation that comes from waiting and sitting with a question. Witnesses are comfortable with the unresolved, uncertain, and in-between seasons of life. We allow questions to remain as questions because we recognize the slow work of sacred movements. If we answer questions too quickly, then we cut off the opportunity for the divine presence around us and within us to respond. Instead, we wait to allow for sacred movements to respond to our questions in their own ways and in their own time. Rather than feeling a need to master and know everything which can be part of a colonizing energy, we consider what can be left unknown.

As a spiritual director, I try to avoid ending a listening session with a sense of resolution or a takeaway. Instead, I often end a session by naming the questions we are holding together in this season. By ending with questions, we get comfortable with the slow and ongoing movements of the sacred. As a witness, however, I can assure those I listen to that I am holding their questions with them as my prayer. And I will companion them as we come back to these questions again and again. Together we witness how our questions slowly evolve over months and years.

Returning to Our Origin

The cyclical way of healing implies not a destination, but a returning to yourself. Western spirituality is often presented as self-improvement and self-help. The intention is a new you or a better you. This Western notion of self-help implies there's something wrong with us that needs to be fixed. A cyclical healing emphasizes that our evolvements are a continual returning to ourselves. At the very center of our cyclical life is our sacred self. In cyclical healing, then, we are not transforming into a new and improved person. We're not looking for a resource outside ourselves. We are accessing what has always been in us already. Daoist, Buddhist, and Hindu practitioners call this a "returning to our origin." Our healing is a coming into our wholeness or completeness. It is experiencing the fullness of who we have always been and already are. As a witness then, I don't dwell on notions that those I witness are flawed or broken even if they think that of themselves. Instead I hold the reality that those I witness are already whole and sacred, until they can return to that knowing themselves.

As I meet with women of color, the journey of returning, however, comes with deep grief. We profoundly notice what's been lost or stolen from us. We've especially lost many of our rituals and cultural traditions. Deconstructing is an ideological movement that's often located in the mind. We may be actively resisting the Western faith we've been given. But deconstructing is impersonal and doesn't recognize the deep grief and real loss of community and safety we've held for so long. Deconstruction can feel like violence to our souls. Often deconstructing leaves a void, and we may feel loneliness and anxiety in trying to fill the void. Entering into a cyclical spirituality recognizes that there are seasons of letting go and seasons of emergence. Letting go means coming to a place of acceptance and peace with the grief and the void. We give ourselves permission to let go of what we've been given. This letting go is not an end; it clears up space in ourselves in order to access the sources within us that we weren't aware of before.

As we grieve what can't be retrieved, we also actively engage what can be reclaimed. Even if we may have lost the particularities of our family's stories, we can still learn about our cultural stories. My role as a witness is to offer a space that helps us recover and reclaim what we can from our cultural spiritualities. Often when we're trying to reconnect with our cultural traditions we ask "what do I do?," "how do I do it?," and "am I doing it right?" But I think there are questions we can ask before the doing. We can ask: "What presence did my cultural ancestors carry in this world?" "What were their rhythms, relational connections, and values that formed their way of being?" These questions help us reclaim the ways of being that inform our cultural rituals and practices. Then when we practice our cultural rituals and traditions imperfectly and awkwardly, we can feel the encouragement of our ancestors who are laughing not at us but with delight and joy for us in our returning.

DECOLONIZING SPIRITUALITY

Trigger Warning: If Practice One is too traumatizing for you, then skip to Practice Two.

Practice One:

Look at your body in front of a mirror. You may choose to look at your naked body if you're comfortable. What do you feel and experience when you look at yourself with a:

- colonizer's gaze;
- missionary gaze;
- patriarchal gaze;
- ableist gaze;
- heteronormative gaze;
- gender binary gaze;
- other gazes you've experienced?

Notice sensations and emotions that arise in you.

Practice Two:

Now shift away from the mirror and away from an outward gaze on your body. Enter into your body and experience your body through touch, movement, and other senses.

Notice what you feel.

Allow your body to tell you who you are.

Colonization was and continues to be acts of injustice, violence, and cruelty toward our Indigenous communities. Colonization and colonialism also created a system of slavery of our African American communities to sustain the insatiable greed of its systems. Colonization is still an active and global force of harm today. At the same time, colonization is a worldview that led to these atrocious acts. A colonizing worldview believes that our natural world is for human utility and consumption. This worldview then easily led to the belief that land and other peoples could be taken and used for our own utility and consumption. Fundamentally, colonization comes from a worldview of ownership, whereas an indigenous worldview does not believe that anyone can own land, people, or our natural world. In a sense, many of us have also embodied this colonizing worldview, which can be seen in the ways we still treat the earth. We perpetuate and maintain systems of colonization. Colonization causes not only physical harm to those treated as commodities, but also causes embodied, internalized, and generational harm both in those oppressed by colonization as well as in those enacting the colonizing. When those enacting or enabling colonization are unable to see the sacredness in another human being or in nature, especially to the point of violence and harm, they experience a distortion of their own sacredness and humanity as well.

Decolonizing then is healing the harm that has been caused, including the layers of physical, economic, systemic, internalized, and generational harm. Decolonizing means proactively uprooting a colonizing worldview, as well as actively engaging in reparations for our Indigenous and Black communities. Decolonizing is not just changing our ideas, understandings, or concepts, but requires a deep undoing of ingrained and embodied Western-centeredness in our actions and ways of being. The decolonizing work looks different for those in oppressed communities versus those that are in communities that have historically been the oppressors. In a collective worldview though there is work that we all need to engage in for healing and restoration. It will take a communal effort to restore harmony to our communities. Contemplative witnessing with BIPOC communities inherently requires addressing the harm of colonization and restoring healing and harmony to communities of color. In the practice of witnessing, decolonizing as a sacred movement might require confronting the internalized Western gaze and unforming the violence of binaries. We then connect with our cultural spiritualities by entering through our bodies.

Confronting the Western Missionary Gaze

I once took a class called "Folk Religions." One of the assignments of this distance course was to observe a non-Christian religious space and record our observations. Already this assignment was centered on the experiences of the white male professor who labeled all religions not his own as "folk" and "primitive." I was living in Taiwan at the time, so to fulfill the assignment I went to a local temple to conduct observations. I felt a strange dissonance as the assignment required me to use my own body to observe my own people as "other," "superstitious," and "folk." I was asked to embody the Western missionary gaze to look at my own people. But in my observations, I didn't see or experience my people as other. All I saw was how beautiful my people are and how meaningful our spiritual practices. So I turned around and left. For my assignment I wrote about how Western evangelicalism is actually a folk religion based on the professor's own parameters of a folk religion.

For BIPOC communities that were raised in the Christian tradition we have internalized the Western missionary gaze in how we look at ourselves and our own cultures. This gaze developed as Western missionaries went into other peoples' lands and encountered difference. These were very physical and visceral experiences of difference, like different sounds, smells, images, tastes, and art, as well as movements. The Western missionaries chose to react to this difference with fear and control. The missionaries then created labels for what was different and unfamiliar to their own cultures, labels like "exotic," "superstitious," "uneducated," and "evil." In order to control what they couldn't understand, the Christian faith and spirituality became equated with Western standards of sounds, smells, images, tastes, and movements.

BIPOC communities have internalized those labels, and that is the Western missionary gaze. We may have been taught that our cultural traditions and practices are sinful or evil. This has caused an internal and embodied disassociation within ourselves. This shows up in a bifurcation of culture from our spirituality. We may not see our own culture as sacred. We may have strong negative reactions to the spiritual practices from our own cultural traditions. For some of us we've lived our whole lives disassociated from ourselves and not known any differently. Chung Hyun Kyung writes in *Struggle to Be the Sun Again*, "oppression makes the oppressed experience separation of self. The oppressed woman experiences a most severe split within herself. The sense of who she wants to be as a human being and her reality of who she is in capitalist/patriarchal society are radically different and opposite, and this situation produces shame, guilt, and self-hate."[9] For some of us, we've had generations of disassociation, perhaps our parents and grandparents also lived disassociated lives in the Christian church. Even if our social context was an ethnic immigrant church, the whole congregation may have internalized the missionary gaze.

A movement of decolonizing is to unform the Western missionary gaze on our bodies and cultures. As a witness I often hear the Western missionary gaze as an internalized criticism or neglect of self. When I ask Asian Americans how their culture influences their spirituality, many don't know how to respond because they've never given themselves permission to integrate these parts of their lives. We need to actively name and identify the Western missionary gaze on our bodies and cultures and be angry at all it's taken from us. We actively release the gaze by experiencing our sacred selves not through how others might perceive us but through feeling and sensing the sacredness of our own bodies.

Unforming Binaries

The Western worldview is built on dichotomies and the inability to hold multiple truths together. The Western way forces a choice. We've been taught that we must choose our religion. If we belonged to one group, then we were not the others. These binaries naturally create othering. For people of color this dichotomy can result in violence to our souls and bodies by asking us to separate and split ourselves. We were forced to reject and neglect the cultural traditions, rituals, and wisdoms of our families. This choice forced a conflict in our identities that didn't actually need to be in conflict.

As a witness I often hear the tension of binaries. The question we've been taught to ask through the Western worldview for entering into a religion is "What are right or wrong beliefs?" This question is first a binary question and second a cognitive question located in the mind. But this question is irrelevant to cultures with nonbinary worldviews that don't experience spirituality through a lens of right and wrong. To reconnect with our cultural traditions, the Western Christian way of entering with the head and beliefs is not the approach. As witnesses we can invite others to release the tension caused by a worldview that forces us to choose.

When I was able to release the binaries passed on to me from the Western Christian tradition, then my experience of God expanded. Taiwan is a spiritually diverse nation. If you were to walk into a Buddhist temple, you would also find Daoist elements, ancestral practices, and other traditions. The ability to hold multiple truths, realities, and spiritualities together has always been the way of my people. I believe this is the reason why Taiwan was the first Asian nation to legalize gay marriage. As a collective, we were open to the many ways in which human beings experience love. Without binaries I can honor all the spiritual and ancestral traditions in my cultural lineage. This includes the Christian tradition in a small Taiwanese immigrant church in the United States, and it includes the ancestral, Daoist, and Buddhist traditions. There is no contradiction in holding all these traditions together. Ancient Chinese philosophers realized that it was impossible for human beings to name or define God because our human vocabulary is limited, so they simply referred to divine presence as the *dao*, which is literally translated as the "the way." They sensed that the divine creator is a way of life that we are invited into. We can experience the divine not only as a noun but as a verb, a divine movement and energy that is constantly active in our lives. These cultural knowings of the divine didn't fit into the box of the Western god. In the Chinese language gods also have their own pronouns not associated with any gender that naturally allow for the divine presence to not be limited by the human conception of gender binaries. Without a need to hold binaries then Jesus can be divine, and God is so expansive that God can express divinity in a diversity of ways.

Entering with Our Bodies

If you were to go to Taiwan and ask people what their religion is, it's most likely that they won't answer with the name of a religion or even with a noun. Instead, it's more likely that you'll hear a verb, *bai bai*. *Bai bai* refers to the practices of maintaining ancestral altars, visiting temples, praying, and other rituals. In the Taiwanese worldview the spiritual and sacred are everywhere and constantly interacting with our physical world. An interactive spiritual realm is reality. There's no need to question its existence or theology with our minds. Instead we engage the spiritual world with our physical bodies.

If Western missionaries started by controlling our bodies, we undo the harm and reclaim our sacredness through our bodies. In contemplative witnessing, then, we can also move away from theological discussion and debate, that is the Western way. Instead, we need to enter with our bodies and experiences. Spirituality is not located in the mind; it is embodied practice and connection to the sacred in our everyday, including the sacred in our cultural traditions. We decolonize by experiencing the dance, the bows, the movements, tastes, sounds, and smells.

My undergraduate degree was in religion and East Asian studies. I've long held a fascination with studying cultures and religions. But I've realized that I've primarily engaged with my mind by trying to study spirituality. In this season of life, I am engaging an intentional shift in my spirituality through annual pilgrimages to sacred spaces. My intention is to learn about spirituality through experience rather than study. Sacred spaces represent the human desire throughout history to experience the transcendent. A sacred space invites us to enter with our bodies first. Through space, art, and ritual, we can engage in spiritual transformation. We allow our bodies to lead and then speak to our souls. Through engaging with interactive sacred spaces, I can intentionally re-form my body through rituals. My body then unforms what I once was taught to perceive as evil.

Contemplative witnesses may facilitate embodied spiritual practices, so I add here a few comments on cultural appropriation. The reason why cultural practices like yoga, tai chi, reiki, mindfulness, and other non-Western spiritual practices have been so easy to culturally appropriate by Western peoples is because Eastern worldviews don't believe that we can own the sacred. It would be preposterous for spiritual teachers to think that the path that led them to the sacred is the only path or that they own the path. So they freely shared what they knew, trusting that each person had their own connections to the divine and that there are many other paths.

Cultural appropriation occurs, then, when a worldview of ownership takes cultural practices not one's own and claims it as their own. Rather than a worldview of ownership, we can engage cultural practices with a worldview of relationship. We can choose to be in relationship with the peoples and cultures that have gifted us a diversity of spiritual practices. To be in an active relationship, then, means that we are advocates for the healing and liberation of those we are building relationship with. We can do this in practical ways like always naming, attributing, and citing where spiritual practices come from. We can honor the relationship by not altering the practices, and particularly not stripping the practice of its original spiritual intentions. Relationships are reciprocal, so we can also ask ourselves "How can I give back?" We can share our finances, access, influence, and power. Susanna Barkataki, in the book *Embracing Yoga's Roots: Courageous Ways to Deepen Your Yoga Practice*, offers intentional practices we can incorporate as facilitators and leaders to avoid cultural appropriation.[10]

三

Our Collective Spirit

What does our communal healing and restoration look like?

As witnesses we need to see people not just as individuals but also in the context of their families, communities, and generations. Whatever is happening in contemplative witnessing, even if powerful and healing, is not complete until the healing is extending to one's relationships. Our individual healing and liberation will always be incomplete and temporary unless we're caring for the collective. Thus as witnesses our concern is not just for individuals but we always carry this collective question: What does our communal healing and restoration look like? As contemplative witnesses we are witnesses to our times. Contemplative witnessing is a commitment to be in spaces of communal grief, lament, suffering, conflict, protest, resistance, pain, and anger. We are asking how we might care for our collective in this moment of history. Thus, we're prepared for the communal crises and hard conversations in our communities. We are ready to provide communal care.

Communal Crises

In the book *Crisis Contemplation*, Barbara Holmes writes about communal crises. She defines communal crises in this way: "Often, a crisis of the community is inflicted by an event, entity, or system. It can be a devastating and destructive divergence from our ordinary lives. Nothing can be learned from a genocide or holocaust other than the human potential for unspeakable cruelty and our ability to survive together."[1] A communal crisis is one in which there is no satisfiable explanation or rationalization for suffering or violence. It is also communal in that a whole community is thrown into the experience together. When in communal crises, contemplative witnesses are those ready to enter in and be present to the community. Our presence doesn't always mean we have solutions, but we can support the community by remaining present to the uncertainty and pain. Barbara Holmes believes that contemplation plays a particular role in these communal crises. She writes, "Contemplation after or during crisis is a stillness in the aftermath of a primal scream, the abyss of unknowing, the necessity of surviving the trauma together."[2] In crisis situations we are equipped to offer spaces of rest, slowing down, and to actively advocate for our collective healing.

Oftentimes communal crises come out of human acts of cruelty and evil. It takes a deep rootedness to not retreat, but to stay present to what's happening. Howard Thurman wisely wrote in *Meditations of the Heart*, "There is no need to fear evil. There is every need to understand what it does, how it operates in the world, what it draws upon to sustain itself."[3] This is the shrewd posture of a contemplative witness. Spirituality without justice is empty. Instead, spirituality is what forms us in a grounded presence to actively address harmful political ideologies, policies, economic exploitations, militaristic values, and other systems of oppression in this world without losing our souls in the process. Our communal rest and healing are dependent on this work. Thurman continues, "Therefore the evil in the world around us must not be allowed to move from without to within."[4] These systems of oppression and violence require not just tactical activism, but also the slow inner work of addressing our callousness, fears, divisiveness, and hatred. These are heart issues as cruelty and violence have distorted our hearts. We need a grounded yet firm presence to address the deepest levels of injustices. We need to be rooted in our sacredness and the sacredness of all humanity and nature.

There are times in which what we witness is not just a news story but is a lived experience. In these times the issues of injustice are not just cognitive, but personal and visceral physical responses. We confront raw and overwhelming emotions. We all have experiences in community in which all we can do to respond is to cry with and to stay with those who are suffering. We are not afraid of these communal crises. We are prepared to enter in, to be present, and not run away.

In May 2022 there was a mass shooting in a Taiwanese immigrant church in Southern California. One person died confronting the shooter head-on to protect the many elderly who were there that day. His sacrifice allowed others to tackle and hold down the shooter. Their actions prevented a greater tragedy. The elderly there that day included my relatives and family friends. These were aunties and uncles that I grew up with in the church. Later on, it was revealed that the shooter was a descendent of Chinese Nationalists, which stirred up historical collective trauma for the Taiwanese elderly there that day who lived under the military rule of the Chinese Nationalist Party for almost four decades from 1949 to 1987.

Just a couple of days before this incident there was a mass shooting at a grocery store in Buffalo, New York, and a week after a shooting at an elementary school in Uvalde, Texas. I was experiencing both a personal grief and a palpable communal grief. In that season I felt raw and couldn't stop crying. I could feel that my tears were not just my own, but generational. I happened to be scheduled to meet with my spiritual director in the same week. I considered cancelling our session because I was a mess. But at the same time, this was exactly the time in which I needed to see my spiritual director. So I showed up for my mess to be witnessed. When I met with her, I couldn't talk much. I mostly just cried for that hour. Even when I tried to speak, what I spoke was incoherent. My body responded when my mind couldn't process. Yet my spiritual director simply remained present. She didn't try to soothe or comfort, but just allowed me to cry. These are exactly the moments that contemplative witnessing is for.

Hard Conversations

As we are witnesses to collective tragedies, our social media lives will push us toward debate and defense. Although these responses may be necessary, they can be very agitating to our spirits. Debate can get violent as well. So when we hold space together as witnesses, we bring the experience down from the head into our hearts and bodies. The people around us may be trying to make our circumstances an issue to discuss, to problem solve, or to plan. We also may be telling ourselves to get over it or move on. In contemplative witnessing we are inviting each other to be present to the pain and the questions. Sikh activist Valarie Kaur, in her book *See No Stranger*, writes on how communal witnessing might help us heal collectively as a nation from the pains of racism and violence. She writes, "It requires witnessing the pain of trauma without trying to control or colonize or minimize it—then listening, and continuing to listen."[5] Kaur teaches us that our role is to allow what we feel to be fully expressed and experienced and to experience with each other.

Whenever I spend time with someone who I know is grieving or suffering, I can feel the resistance and tension in myself because I know it'll be hard. I'd rather not be there as I want to avoid the feelings of helplessness and uncertainty. But then I remind myself that this is what I was trained for. When we witness pain in others our first tendency is often to figure out how to help. Our motivation for helping, however, may come from wanting to relieve the discomfort and tensions we feel in ourselves. A helping energy is dependent on ourselves. Instead of asking ourselves "how do I help?," we might ask ourselves "how might I offer a healing and restful presence?"

We can also cause harm with hope. Oftentimes, if we're uncomfortable or uncertain of how to respond to someone, we may respond with statements of hope or we ask questions trying to lead the other to hope. We want some sort of feeling of resolution in the uncertainty. Statements of hope, however, can end the conversation. Hope can cause the person being witnessed to feel that their pain and reality was dismissed or disregarded. Forcing hope communicates that there's no space for what we feel.

Therefore, as witnesses we are prepared to facilitate spaces of grief and lament. We live in a modern culture that does not know how to grieve or how to face death or endings. As a community we often respond with words of comfort. In the practice of contemplative witnessing, however, those that are grieving don't need more words of comfort. Instead they need to grieve fully. We experience grief, for example, when we experience a loss beyond our mental comprehension and there are no words to explain. Instead, grief is a very visceral and embodied emotion. Contemplative witnesses provide grief space by becoming comfortable with feeling uncomfortable. The practices of anger, lament, and grief leave the unresolved as unresolved, leave uncertainty as uncertainty, leave questions as questions. Sometimes this means being willing to be present as someone cries for an hour. We witness the tears, and we don't have to do anything more than that. We also create space for the longevity of grief. Oftentimes our communities support us through acts of care when a grief is fresh, but then they move on with their lives and expect the grievers to do the same. Contemplative witnesses, on the other hand, companion us through all the cycles of grief as the grief evolves over months, years, and decades. We can collectively hold each other's griefs, pains, or anger without dismissing or needing to resolve difficult emotions.

Sometimes if we continue to ask questions, we may be asking those we witness to try and explain and understand something that just simply isn't explicable. There are no words to rationalize acts of cruelty or hate. Evil is evil. Violence is violence. Injustice is injustice. There are times when our questions can actually cause harm. When we ask questions and expect answers we may be forcing someone to explain something that can't be explained, rationalize something that isn't rational, to find hope when there is no hope.

We may end up pushing those we witness to somehow come up with words to explain what's happening when there are no words. We may be pushing those we witness to tolerate injustice. We may end up expecting people to say phrases like "I should just trust God more" or "I'm supposed to learn a lesson from this experience." Those kinds of optimistic phrases can close the conversation. They may be suppression and survival techniques.

Instead of asking the next question in those times, it may be helpful to pull away from words. Stop and feel without needing to put words to it. Our goal is not to understand our anger, but to feel our anger, and to not cut off the tears, but to cry together. Through witnessing we learn to feel together in a culture that taught us not to. So a powerful practice is to create space just to feel what we feel without judgment, rationalizing, or trying to find hope, and to feel together in community. Witnesses are not afraid of difficult emotions. Difficult emotions are not enemies or something wrong with us. They are just ways our bodies are communicating with us. Witnesses help us attend to these emotions.

Anger, lament, and grief are communal spiritual practices. As witnesses we can't be scared away and we can't be quick to soothe just because we're uncomfortable. Instead we join the communal practice. By sharing in the emotions, we are expressing that the issues or problems are not your problems but ours. When we cry with and rage with, then racial issues are not isolated incidents, but our collective and shared responsibility.

Collective Sacred Movements

Our sacred movements are not only individual, we also have collective sacred movements. These are movements that bring healing to our collective spirit and our collective body. Decolonizing is only part of the work. It is simply an undoing and restoring. We also need a way forward, which means living into a healing way of being in community. For BIPOC communities to always have to fight against injustice and racism is exhausting. To care for our collective in communal crises and hard conversations is also heavy. Liberation is when we start to move toward what we're for and the spirituality and community we need. Some sacred movements can't be done alone, they are experienced collectively. The two collective movements that follow are generational healing in our families and restoring harmony in our communities.

GENERATIONAL HEALING

Practice:

Ancestral practices are often mutual receiving and giving of blessings and prayers. Through these practices we receive the blessings of our ancestors while also offering our blessings and prayers for them in their afterlife.

In what ways are blessings given and received in your own culture or family? How might you incorporate objects, rituals, or foods of blessing into your spiritual practice as a witness?

I once had a session with my spiritual director in which I talked about my day at the DMV. For non-US readers, the Department of Motor Vehicles (DMV) is where we test and apply for our driver's license and also the place we register our vehicles. The DMV has the reputation of long lines and several hours of waiting. Such was my experience at the DMV that day, especially after computer systems suddenly shut down and we waited an additional hour for the computers to be restored again. What drew my attention that day, however, were the non-English-speaking first-generation immigrants trying to navigate the complex DMV system. I observed people frustrated with not having the right forms and needing to leave only to come back another day and start in line all over again. My heart and compassion also went out to the Spanish- and Chinese-speaking employees patiently helping confused customers. Something stirred within me as I remembered my childhood self in that space. I remember navigating the complex US public school system in order to translate for my parents and tell them what they should do as parents. So, when I started the conversation with my spiritual director with "So, I went to the DMV this week . . .," I needed my childhood self as a child of immigrants to be witnessed.

In my book *Our Unforming* I wrote a chapter on multigenerational living and how it was essential to my formation. I wrote about the beautiful cyclical practice of my parents taking care of my grandparents while my grandparents took care of me. But one of the common reactions I received, especially from Asian Americans, was how triggering and even traumatic it is to be around their parents. I understand their pains, and regret that I did not address those pains. The hard work of intergenerational healing is also a sacred movement that comes with additional layers of complexities for communities of color. These sacred movements might engage with traumas from war, immigration, migration, poverty, slavery, genocide, and so on. And a real grief is that not everyone has the opportunity of being able to engage with the parents, grandparents, or elders they've lost, or their elders may be unwilling or incapable to engage with healing movements.

For some of us, our elders have passed away and we can't have the conversations we wish we could have had. Perhaps our elders were abusive, and we choose for our well-being not to engage with our lineage. The trauma of migration and immigration may be another part of the story. Our elders may have intentionally or unintentionally disconnected themselves from their culture and their past. Cross-cultural or transnational adoptees also may be cut off from access to their ancestry and culture. The only response for what's lost is grief and lament. There's a reality that we can't get it back. We need to grieve fully. Our modern culture has made grieving really isolated, but grief is meant to be a communal practice. Barbara Holmes writes in *Crisis Contemplation*, "We have to admit that we have been broken before we can be healed. We can't heal until we can grieve the events that have wounded us, release the spiritual toxins left behind, and open ourselves to something new. Communal grieving offers something that we cannot get when we grieve by ourselves."[6] We need to be witnessed in our grief. The role of the community is not to bring any sense of resolve. But what the community can do is acknowledge. We can acknowledge how we feel, acknowledge who or what we've lost, and witness who we are with a part of ourselves missing.

If our intention is not to resolve the grief, then we can acknowledge through grieving rituals. Ancestral altars are one example of a grief ritual. What Western missionaries saw as idol worship is actually an embodied grief practice. Maintaining a family altar involves creating rhythms of communal grieving. Each time we come to the altar we recognize that our grief doesn't go away, but that our grief may change and evolve over time.

I experienced something new when I started meeting directees who are first-generation immigrants to the United States. Conversations with them remind me of conversations with my parents, aunties, and uncles. I could recognize familiar survival mechanisms like frugality or the legalistic need for rigidity and guardrails that give a sense of safety. They can be strict and harsh with themselves. But because they are engaging in intentional spiritual direction, it also reminds me that sometimes our elders can choose healing.

I'm not a therapist and I don't have clear answers on how we might engage in healthy relationships with our elders, but the following four postures have been helpful for me. These postures are ancestral practices, honoring our experiences, loving detachment, and compassionate presence. These intentional postures are cyclical as generational healing occurs before us, through our lifetimes, and beyond us. A question that my spiritual director asked me to consider is "What are the invitations for me in this generation?" We may be invited into generational healing if we feel we have more capacity than the generations before us.

Ancestral Practices

To engage in generational healing we must connect to the generations before us. These may be familial ancestors known and unknown, but can also be cultural or spiritual ancestors. Facilitating a connection back to our ancestral lineage, cultures, and spirituality, however, may require a worldview shift for some of us. Ancestral practices begin with a worldview that believes in the active presence of spirits. This is a worldview often lost in the Western world. Our ancestors are present with us. They are not limited by time or physical boundaries. If we have a worldview that believes in the lived presence of our ancestors, then there is a connection. We believe then that our ancestors can communicate to us through dreams, through felt senses, through symbols, and rituals. We believe that our ancestors can participate with us in our generational healing even in their afterlife. Our ancestors are the community of witnesses that believe in us. They believe we have the sources of healing within us and in our own cultures, even if we're unaware. What we're searching for is not outside of us, but we already have access to healing resources. We can connect to our ancestors that passed down to us a life-giving spirituality and ways of being. We equally have in our lineage ancestors that may have been violent or ancestors that were oppressors. Generational healing requires confronting all these stories of our past. For our ancestors that were abusive or harmful, we pray that they have confronted their wrongs in the next life and we openly name and address their misdeeds in this life as part of our responsibilities in this generation.

Honoring Our Experiences

For communities of color, oftentimes the trauma we experience in our families is generational trauma. So a movement of healing is to acknowledge the historical traumas our elders may have experienced. We also honor their resilience and the ways that they tried to survive. The generations before us may not have had the capacity for an introspective life. They may have lived a lifetime of suppression. They didn't have the same access to mental health resources or other healing sources. They have strong defense mechanisms that they needed for their survival. If they spent the first sixty years of their life living with these survival mechanisms, then it may take sixty years to heal from those ingrained mechanisms.

Acknowledging the trauma and wounds of our elders doesn't lessen our own. We also equally acknowledge the hurt, neglect, or abuse we experienced or continue to experience from elders who projected their traumas onto us in various ways. We honor our own resilience and survival. All can be true at the same time. But now we may have access to more healing resources so we can make a choice to engage our generational healing for ourselves and for our elders and ancestors who couldn't. Even if our elders refuse their own healing, we still have the choice to engage the hard work of our own healing which includes addressing the traumas that our elders may be unable to face themselves.

An important communal practice for BIPOC communities is to speak our families' stories. We must speak our immigration stories, our war stories, our resistance stories, our survival stories. Our speaking out before a community of witnesses may be unforming the silence of generations. We may have grown up in families and cultures in which traumatic or negative experiences are suppressed and ignored. Thus for our generational healing there are times in which we must speak on behalf of our parents, grandparents, and ancestors who may not have had the opportunity to speak their stories. Although we may not always know their individual stories, we know the historical contexts in which they lived. As a spiritual practice, we continually remember and speak our historical and communal stories. Speaking our truths, past and present, as BIPOC communities is foundational for our communal healing.

Desmond Tutu wrote of the Truth and Reconciliation Commissions in South Africa, "In the end only an honest confrontation with reality can bring real healing. Superficial reconciliation can bring only superficial healing."[7] Truth commissions facilitate a communal speaking and witnessing on a national scale in order to confront the realities of injustice, violence, and trauma. Truth commissions demonstrate the healing power of speaking our experiences and stories as an intentional collective practice. As a collective the United States, however, has not been willing to listen to or confront our ugly truths of slavery, colonization, and genocide. Consequently, we continue to perpetuate cycles of racism and violence by trying to move on without addressing our pasts. We need to communally confront our truths, even if hard and uncomfortable, in order to enter our collective healing and liberation. A collective generational healing includes addressing our historical societal traumas and not just the traumas in our families of origin.

Loving Detachment

The most loving thing we can do in intergenerational healing is to pursue our own healing and well-being. In the end, we can't force inner work on anybody else, we can only engage our own healing. We also can't change people unless they themselves decide to change. But when we engage our own healing, we invite others into their healing too.

Therapists may emphasize the importance of self-differentiation in difficult relationships. Self-differentiation is actually an ancient practice called detachment or nonattachment. It refers to the ability to let the emotions and reactivities of others to be their own, without us absorbing or being responsible for them. At the same time, we are attuned to and responsible for our own emotions and reactivities. For abusive elders, although their energy may be directed at us, their reactivity is actually about themselves, their own fears, anxieties, and wounds. Their critical and judgmental voice, directed at us, often means the way they speak to themselves is likely even more critical and harsh. If we become reactive when our elders are reactive, that doesn't help anyone. Rather we need to find our own grounded presence and peace to offer a peaceful presence to our family members. Reactivity comes out of not being able to look at ourselves. We cultivate a healthy detachment through practices of mindfulness and attentiveness. This is deeply inner work and not just relational work. Loving detachment may mean seasons in which we leave or don't engage with our family members for a while until we engage our own healing first, for however long healing may take. Sometimes that healing season is for the rest of our lives. Sometimes we allow the next generation to heal for us if we feel we don't have the capacity in this generation.

Compassionate Presence

When and if we are ready, we may engage with our elders again with compassionate presence. It's possible that our elders have never offered compassion and love to themselves. They may have lived most of their lives with harsh external and internal voices. You may be the first and only compassionate and loving voice they will ever hear. This may mean that they are conditioned to reject your love, care, and compassion. They may literally try to push that affection away. But I believe they do notice. I remind myself that a little bit of emotional expression to us may be a lot to them if they are not used to acknowledging their emotions. Their resistance and hardness is like a wall, and needs continual tenderness and care to soften and break through. It may be slow or impossible work, but our small acts of love, kindness, and affection are intentional practices. We never know when an act of compassion will break through.

It also takes small intentional practices to unform survival mechanisms like frugality. We can love our elders by helping them enjoy the simple things in life like going out to eat, traveling, and trying new things. As a child I grew more and more distant from my dad because of his constant criticism and anger. As an adult my relationship with my dad shifted when I realized that he's actually anxious and scared, but he lived in an environment where men couldn't express their fears because that was considered weak. I realized that any changes made him especially anxious, so he was highly resistant to trying new things and anything different than the security of his routine. When I began to see my dad's anxiety, I was then able to extend compassion each time he reacted with criticism. My dad still often resists with grumpiness and complaints, but I'm different. I choose to believe he's quietly appreciative on the inside. When my dad enjoys something he says "not bad" and I have learned that's actually the highest compliment he gives, so I receive it that way. In the same way that we would like community to allow us to change and to witness our changes, if we have capacity then we might give our elders the same grace that they can change too, whether they choose to or not.

Gathering Communal Resources

We have inherited not just generational trauma, healing resources have been passed down to us too. Elders that spent their lives in survival mode don't know what to do when their survival mechanisms are no longer needed. Everyone likes being needed and valued, and even more so as we age and question our usefulness. Asking our elders for their help is an invitation to community. It communicates that they are needed in community even if they complain as they help. Asking our elders for help can draw out their communal knowledge and experiences. For our elders that are resistant and hesitant to tell their stories, then we can begin by drawing from their skills.

Celebrating and eating together has always been a healing spiritual practice for our families and communities. These gatherings can give momentary relief from the hard work of communicating and healing relationships. Rest for first-generation immigrants is to have spaces where they can take a break from navigating unfamiliar systems. There is a unique sense of rest that we receive when we can fully be ourselves in the contexts of our communities and not have to explain our ways of being. We need places for our cultural spiritualities, rituals, and traditions to be welcomed, centered, and celebrated. We need spaces where we can relax our tense and weary muscles. This too is part of our generational healing.

RESTORING HARMONY

Practice:

Open up your attunements to our collective.

What senses or emotions can you feel that are not just your own, but collective?

Bring your shared emotion or sense into your space of prayer or meditation.

Allow your collective attunement to teach you about what the collective needs.

This last year I spent a month in Taiwan to learn tai chi. I wanted to experience spirituality through my own body and through movement. I found a teacher, a man around my age who had studied traditional Chinese and Taiwanese practices in university. Every other day we met at a public garden in southern Taiwan for an hour. I was surprised in our very first lesson, however, when the hour flew past and at the end of the lesson I realized that we spent the entire hour on simply learning how to breathe and how to stand. I was not aware that I didn't know how to breathe or stand. My teacher said something in that first lesson that I continue to dwell on.

He said that when we are centered and aligned in our most natural stance, then we may not notice or feel anything at all. Everything is working as it should and flowing smoothly. It's only when we are misaligned or imbalanced that we may start to notice a tension, pressure, a strain. And if we don't notice or if we choose to ignore those small pressures, then over time what once was slight can become aches and pains in our body. I realized that learning how to breathe and stand was inviting me to learn a foundation of what healing, health, and harmony feels like in my own body, in my life, and in our communities.

This principle of sensing the imbalances and tensions is a foundation for Daoist spirituality and Eastern medicine. When an Eastern medicine doctor treats a person holistically the main question they are asking is what is not in harmony? So as doctors they don't just ask questions about the body, they also ask questions about our emotions, our family life, our work life, and where we live. And they are listening for tensions, pressures, blockages, and misalignments in our lives. A holistic view of healing means that we live in a mutual and symbiotic relationship with everything, with the divine, with the natural world, with spirits, with each other in community, with our emotions, and within our own bodies. All of these are interrelated and interconnected. It begins in our physical bodies with the harmony of our organs, breath, and blood. Every movement and every food or nutrient we consume affects the harmony in our bodies. Overindulgence can create imbalances. The harmony in our bodies affects the harmony of our emotions, and vice versa. If there's pressure or disruption in one area, perhaps tensions in a relationship, it will create tensions in other areas, perhaps causing illness. Extended and prolonged disruptions can lead to chronic illnesses and pains.

When we embody our role as contemplative witnesses we may be asking the same question: What is not in harmony? We learn to sense misalignments, pressures, and tensions. We attune ourselves to how everything is connected. As witnesses this means we pay attention to everything, including an ache in our body, seasons of sleeplessness, or relational conflicts. All of these can affect our emotional and spiritual well-being. Harmony as a collective sacred movement cannot be attained alone, it requires also attuning ourselves to the community, including our nature community. We can also ask this question collectively: What is not in harmony in our communities?

Collective Attunement

Western self-care often mentions the importance of balance. Western understanding of balance, however, often carries with it a Western worldview of binary thinking. And so we often think of balance as a scale and that everything needs to be equal to achieve balance. A Western notion of balance also tends to be individualistic and dependent on our own efforts to achieve balance. Our binary thinking leads us to believe then that "if I'm doing one thing then I'm not doing another thing," and we feel stress and tension from our scarcity and our limitations. Harmony, on the other hand, is a collective understanding of balance. Harmony as a way of being is fundamental to Daoist spirituality. Indigenous theologian Randy Woodley also writes about the harmony way as an indigenous way of being in his book *Shalom and the Community of Creation*.[8] A posture of harmony recognizes the complexity of our bodies, our human systems, as well as the natural world, but believes in the possibility of synchronicity and attunement to one another.

The natural world is our greatest teacher in living in harmony. In a thriving ecosystem, every being or entity is interconnected and attuned to each other. And if there's disruption or tension in one part of the ecosystem then the other parts feel it too. The other parts of the ecosystem may then extend care and try their best to bring back balance or harmony to the whole. But this harmony is not an either/or binary balance. If there are resources in one part of the ecosystem that doesn't mean there aren't resources in another, instead it requires the diversity of the ecosystem to share resources in order to bring harmony to the whole. We too are technically part of the same ecosystem. But perhaps we have cut ourselves off from our attunements to the whole.

Contemplative witnessing requires us to open up our attunements to the collective. We are made to live in harmony. Certain people have attunement gifts, such as empaths and highly sensitive people. But I do wonder if these gifts are actually supposed to be the norm rather than exceptions, and that it's the rest of society that has cut ourselves off from our attunements. As witnesses we can intentionally open up our attunements to another human being. We can feel and experience one another's emotions. We can also open our attunements to the greater society. Sometimes what we feel is our own response, but other times what we're experiencing are actually our connections to the collective. Our emotions are actually shared emotions. What is happening nationally or globally can naturally affect our well-being. As healers we intentionally learn to sense the tensions, misalignments, and imbalances in our collective, rather than numb our attunements. This requires confronting harm, violence, and injustices because they disrupt our collective harmony.

Indigenous spirituality teaches us we can also be attuned to our nature kin. *Nature kin* is an indigenous term that emphasizes our intimate relationship to nature.[9] Our surrounding nature community are our witnesses too. They have been witnessing us for centuries. They can testify to our best and worst moments as human beings. So immersing in nature is also an intentional act. We can mutually witness our nature community in their suffering and the injustices they experience under human abuse and violence.

Communal Awareness

Western spiritual writers have written about the harm of a dualistic worldview, but the only term they could think of to describe an alternative to a dualistic worldview is *nondualism*. Nondualism is an empty English word because it simply means *not* dualist.

Non-Western cultures that can naturally hold multiple realities and live in relationship with the contradictions and complexities of life raise their children in our interconnectedness. The alternative of dualism isn't nondualism, rather an alternative worldview is our interconnectedness. If we can recognize that all things are interrelated, then we can more naturally hold the multiple realities and truths of life. There are rarely clear binaries, rather there is a recognition that in seasons of joy there can simultaneously be loss. In seasons of grief and pain, there can also be laughter. We often desire clear binaries of good and evil because it gives us a sense of certainty for own lives and beliefs. Binaries allow us to demonize others and see ourselves as pure. Contemplative witnesses are those able to hold the tensions that multiple realities can exist at the same time, and not feel the need to resolve or relieve those tensions. As healers we hold those tensions for ourselves as well as for our communities. Embracing our interconnectedness is what allows us to address the complexities of our broken social systems that often carry multiple stories and pains at the same time.

As those that hold our interconnectedness, we can engage in the practice of communal awareness like we do self-awareness. Communal awareness is a healthy and honest assessment of our collective well-being. We can sense when there's collective anxiety, collective sleeplessness, or collective despair. As a witness there are seasons in which I notice several people describing the same feeling or phenomenon. Like an ecosystem, we know that when there's pain in one community then the rest of us can feel it too. The response of the community is to send support and resources to restore the whole. But our broken social systems are not yet a healthy, thriving ecosystem. There are obstructions and misalignments in our organizations and social systems.

Witnesses as community healers means that our path of activism is through our intentional practices of communal attunement and awareness. We sense the imbalances, disconnections, and obstructions when our connections to one another are disrupted. We call out and name when one part of the collective is harming another. As healers, we can encourage our communities to open up our attunements to another again, to feel together, and to move into the rhythm of a collective harmony.

Conclusion

After my spiritual direction students learn some of the foundational movements of contemplative witnessing, I then free them to explore what this practice looks like and feels like in their own bodies and in their own cultures. Spiritual direction doesn't have to look like the ways we've been trained, especially for BIPOC communities. We each need to learn what it feels like when we embody a healing presence in ourselves and how we each uniquely facilitate healing spaces for our communities. The possibilities of creative spiritual direction and care are endless. We can draw from our ancestral and cultural traditions, and we can also create and imagine new ways to expand our practice. For me this has meant embracing a Daoist way of being and Eastern medicine as healing traditions in my own lineage and drawing from these healing practices to expand my practice of spiritual direction.

I believe that contemplative witnesses are to be the leaders of our times. We live in a modern culture that does not often value the practices of introspection, self-awareness, or communal awareness. This avoidance of the inner life has led to repetitive moral failures in leadership and to our divided, violent societies. We are living in fractured communities and families because we operate out of our reactive, unexamined selves. We need new paradigms of contemplative communal engagement for our times. We need healers, listeners, wise elders, and spiritual guides to be the leaders of our times so that the healing of our inner lives informs our engagement in community. Just like we engage in our inner work and healing, contemplative witnesses can lead us in our collective work and healing. Contemplative leaders can invite us into a different way of being, which includes a different way of leading organizations and communities.

I end with an invitation for spiritual companions and contemplative witnesses to join the lineage of spiritual healers and teachers of our cultural traditions. When we embrace our role as healers in community we join a long line of sages, medicine doctors, shamans, gurus, grandmothers, and elders. These wisdom figures modeled for us the essential role of those that serve as healers and leaders for the collective. This book is named *Contemplative Witnessing* to recognize that our spirituality is always in community. Collective sacred movements require new imaginations, creative solutions, and generativity. As witnesses we can facilitate communal imagination to empower those we witness to see what healing and restoration looks like for their families, organizations, and communities. Imagination is a magical spiritual practice. We may long for a community that we can feel, but may not have the words for yet. But if we can long for it, see it, and feel it, then we can collectively work toward it.

Notes

ACKNOWLEDGMENTS

1 Sherry Bryant-Johnson, Therese Taylor-Stinson, and Rosalie Norman McNaney, eds., *Embodied Spirits: Stories of Spiritual Directors of Color* (Harrisburg, PA: Church Publishing, 2014); Ineda Pearl Adesanya, ed., *Kaleidoscope: Broadening the Palette in the Art of Spiritual Direction* (New York: Church Publishing, 2019).

INTRODUCTION

1 Howard Thurman, "The Sound of the Genuine," address given at the Spelman College Baccalaureate Ceremony, May 4, 1980.

— CONTEMPLATIVE WITNESSING

1 Chung Hyun Kyung, *Struggle to Be the Sun Again: Introducing Asian Women's Theology* (Maryknoll, NY: Orbis Books, 1994), 42.

2 Pamela Ayo Yetunde, *Casting Indra's Net: Fostering Spiritual Kinship and Community: Wisdom from Buddhism, Christianity, Judaism, Hinduism, and More* (Boulder, CO: Shambhala, 2023), 107.

二 SACRED MOVEMENTS

1 Angel Kyodo Williams, Rod Owens, and Jasmine Syedullah, *Radical Dharma: Talking Race, Love, and Liberation* (Berkeley: North Atlantic Books, 2016), 54.
2 Adapted from Grace Ji-Sun Kim, *The Holy Spirit, Chi, and Other* (New York: Palgrave Macmillan, 2011), 12.
3 Therese Taylor-Stinson and Paula Owens Parker, "Internal Liberation," in *Kaleidoscope: Broadening the Palette in the Art of Spiritual Direction*, ed. Ineda Pearl Adesanya (New York: Church Publishing, 2019), 153–76.
4 John Wu, *Chinese Humanism and Christian Spirituality* (Brooklyn: Angelico Press, 2017), 63.
5 Thich Nhat Hanh, Mindfulness Essentials Series (New York: Penguin Random House).
6 Barbara Holmes, *Joy Unspeakable: Contemplative Practices of the Black Church* (Minneapolis: Fortress Press, 2017), 17.
7 Adapted from Thomas Merton, *The Way of Chuang Tzu* (New York: New Directions, 2010), 52.
8 Derek Lin, trans., *Tao Te Ching: Annotated and Explained* (Woodstock, VT: Skylight Paths Publishing, 2009), 126.
9 Chung Hyun Kyung, *Struggle to Be the Sun Again* (Maryknoll, NY: Orbis Books, 1994), 41.
10 Susanna Barkataki, *Embracing Yoga's Roots: Courageous Ways to Deepen Your Yoga Practice* (Orlando: Ignite Yoga and Wellness Institute, 2020).

三 OUR COLLECTIVE SPIRIT

1 Barbara Holmes, *Crisis Contemplation: Healing the Wounded Village* (Albuquerque: CAC Publishing, 2021), 23.
2 Holmes, *Crisis Contemplation*, 45.
3 Howard Thurman, *Meditations of the Heart* (Boston: Beacon Press), 110.
4 Thurman, *Meditations of the Heart*, 111.
5 Valarie Kaur, *See No Stranger: A Memoir and Manifesto of Revolutionary Love* (New York: One World, 2020), 58.
6 Holmes, *Crisis Contemplation*, 108.
7 Desmond Tutu, "Truth and Reconciliation," *Greater Good Magazine*, September 1, 2004, https://greatergood.berkeley.edu/article/item/truth_and_reconciliation.
8 Randy Woodley, *Shalom and the Community of Creation: An Indigenous Vision* (Grand Rapids, MI: Eerdmans, 2012).
9 Jessica Hernandez, *Fresh Banana Leaves: Healing Indigenous Landscapes through Indigenous Science* (Berkeley: North Atlantic Books, 2022), 115.